50 Walks in

GLASGOW & SOUTH WEST SCOTLAND

First published 2003
Researched and written by Hugh Taylor and Moira McCrossan

Produced by AA Publishing
© Automobile Association Developments Limited 2003
Illustrations © Automobile Association Developments Limited 2003

Published by AA Publishing (a trading name of Automobile
Association Developments Limited, whose registered office is
Millstream, Maidenhead, Windsor, SL4 5GD;
registered number 1878835)

ISBN 0 7495 3625 X

A01300

A CIP catalogue record for this book is available
from the British Library.

Visit the AA Publishing website at www.theAA.com

Paste-up and editorial by Outcrop Publishing Services Ltd, Cumbria
for AA Publishing

Colour reproduction by LC Repro
Printed in Italy by G Canale & C SPA, Torino, Italy

Legend

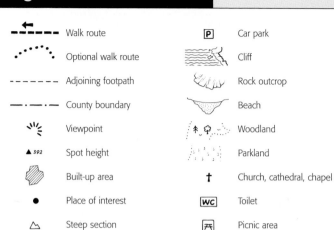

←- - - - -	Walk route	P	Car park
••••••••	Optional walk route		Cliff
- - - - - -	Adjoining footpath		Rock outcrop
—·—·—	County boundary		Beach
☼	Viewpoint		Woodland
▲ 392	Spot height		Parkland
	Built-up area	†	Church, cathedral, chapel
●	Place of interest	WC	Toilet
△	Steep section	禾	Picnic area

Glasgow & South West Scotland locator map

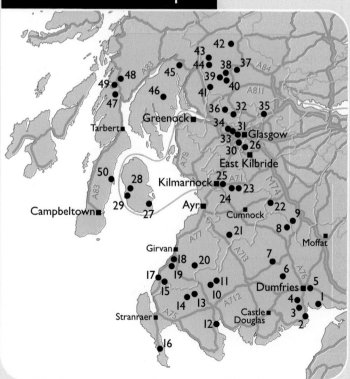

Contents
==================

Contents

WALK	RATING	DISTANCE	PAGE
1 Caerlaverock Castle and the Solway Merses	🚶🚶🚶	5¼ miles (8.4km)	8
2 The Solway Shore from Carsethorn to Arbigland	🚶🚶🚶	5½ miles (8.8km)	11
3 Criffel and New Abbey	🚶🚶🚶	3¾ miles (6km)	14
4 Knochendoch to New Abbey	🚶🚶🚶	7¾ miles (12.5km)	17
5 A Dumfries Town Trail	🚶🚶🚶	5½ miles (8.8km)	18
6 The Glenkiln Outdoor Sculptures	🚶🚶🚶	4 miles (6.4km)	20
7 The Last Turning in Moniaive	🚶🚶🚶	5 miles (8km)	23
8 Wanlockhead: Scotland's Highest Village	🚶🚶🚶	3¾ miles (6km)	26
9 Leadhills Library	🚶🚶🚶	7¼ miles (11.7km)	29
10 The Battle of Glentrool	🚶🚶🚶	5 miles (8km)	30
11 Cycling on the Merrick	🚶🚶🚶	9 miles (14.5km)	32
12 On the Trail of the Wigtown Martyrs	🚶🚶🚶	4 miles (6.4km)	35
13 The Wells of the Rees	🚶🚶🚶	6¼ miles (10.1km)	38
14 The Standing Stones of Laggangarn	🚶🚶🚶	2½ miles (4km)	41
15 Castle Kennedy Gardens	🚶🚶🚶	6 miles (9.7km)	42
16 Port Logan or Fictional Ronansay?	🚶🚶🚶	3 miles (4.8km)	44
17 Ardstinchar Castle	🚶🚶🚶	3 miles (4.8km)	47
18 Byne Hill and the Firth of Clyde	🚶🚶🚶	3¾ miles (6km)	50
19 Kilranny Hill and Steading	🚶🚶🚶	4¼ miles (6.8km)	53
20 Up the Howe of Laggan	🚶🚶🚶	8 miles (12.9km)	54
21 Discover Dunaskin Iron Works	🚶🚶🚶	4 miles (6.4km)	56
22 On Old Roads and Rails Around Muirkirk	🚶🚶🚶	3½ miles (5.7km)	59
23 Darvel Byways	🚶🚶🚶	7 miles (11.3km)	62
24 And on to Newmilns	🚶🚶🚶	11½ miles (18.5km)	65
25 The River Irvine Walk	🚶🚶🚶	7½ miles (12.1km)	66
26 The Museum of Scottish Country Life	🚶🚶🚶	5 miles (8km)	68
27 The Spectacular Falls at Glenashdale	🚶🚶🚶	2¾ miles (4.4km)	71

Contents

WALK		RATING	DISTANCE	PAGE
28	Machrie Moor	🚶🚶 🚶 🚶	5½ miles (8.8km)	74
29	Robert the Bruce	🚶🚶 🚶🚶 🚶	5½ miles (8.8km)	77
30	Glasgow's Architecture	🚶🚶 🚶 🚶	2½ miles (4km)	78
31	Alexander 'Greek' Thomson	🚶🚶 🚶🚶 🚶	6½ miles (10.4km)	80
32	The Carbeth Hut Community	🚶🚶 🚶 🚶	3 miles (4.8km)	83
33	Glasgow Harbour's Tall Ship	🚶🚶 🚶 🚶	4¾ miles (7.7km)	86
34	The Clyde Walkway	🚶🚶 🚶 🚶	5¾ miles (9.2km)	89
35	The Antonine Wall and the Forth and Clyde Canal	🚶🚶 🚶 🚶	3½ miles (5.7km)	90
36	Exploring the Whangie	🚶🚶 🚶🚶 🚶	2½ miles (4km)	92
37	Through the Queen Elizabeth Forest Park	🚶🚶 🚶🚶 🚶	4 miles (6.4km)	95
38	The Great Forest of Loch Ard	🚶🚶 🚶 🚶	3½ miles (5.7km)	98
39	And on to the Duchray Estate	🚶🚶 🚶🚶 🚶	6 miles (9.7km)	101
40	Up the Doon Hill	🚶🚶 🚶🚶 🚶	2 miles (3.2km)	102
41	A Trail Through the Sallochy Woods	🚶🚶 🚶 🚶	2 miles (3.2km)	104
42	From Balquhidder to Creag an Tuirc	🚶🚶 🚶🚶 🚶	2½ miles (4km)	107
43	The Shores of Loch Katrine	🚶🚶 🚶🚶 🚶	6¾ miles (10.9km)	110
44	And on to Loch Dhu and Loch Chon	🚶🚶 🚶🚶 🚶	6 miles (9.7km)	113
45	Rest and Be Thankful	🚶🚶 🚶 🚶	4½ miles (7.2km)	114
46	From Puck's Glen to the Benmore Botanic Garden	🚶🚶 🚶 🚶	4 miles (6.4km)	116
47	Along the Crinan Canal and Around Mhoine Mhor	🚶🚶 🚶🚶 🚶	8¼ miles (13.3km)	119
48	The Neolithic Monuments of Kilmartin Glen	🚶🚶 🚶 🚶	3½ miles (5.7km)	122
49	On To New Poltalloch	🚶🚶 🚶🚶 🚶	6¼ miles (10.1km)	125
50	Carradale Forest Walk	🚶🚶 🚶 🚶	6 miles (9.7km)	126

Rating: Each walk is rated for its relative difficulty compared to the other walks in this book. Walks marked 🚶🚶 🚶 🚶 are likely to be shorter and easier with little total ascent. The hardest walks are marked 🚶🚶 🚶🚶 🚶🚶 .

Walking in Safety: For advice and safety tips ➤ 128.

Introducing Glasgow & South West Scotland

The quiet south west is a good place to start exploring Scotland, from the gently rolling pastures of Dumfriesshire to 'Grey Galloway' with its windswept moors, secluded byways and the rugged Galloway Hills. There are walks in these hills that are every bit as remote and taxing as anything you'll encounter in the Highlands but without the height. The Southern Uplands Way, from Port Patrick in the far west, cuts across the grain of the country and is probably the most difficult long distance footpath in Scotland. Tramp a section of this across open moor and you'll quickly realise why the hill folk of the south west were such a hardy breed.

Cross into Ayrshire and rugged Galloway fades into a pastoral landscape. The coastline of the west is bordered by fertile fields, created from raised beaches, famous for their early potatoes. Once the entire county was covered in moor and bog.

Agricultural improvements and extensive drainage in the 17th and 18th centuries created today's farmland. Inland, and in remote parts of the county, areas of bog and moor still exist. It was from bleak land like this that subsistence farmers and miners scratched a living. Yet many who became household names came from this background. Farmer's son, Alexander Fleming went on to discover penicillin while miner, Bill Shankly, who learned his sporting skills in the village of Glenbuck, became a footballing legend.

Ayrshire gives way to Glasgow and the central belt. The City of Glasgow has risen from the ashes of soot-blackened slums to become the greatest shopping experience north of London. It also revels in the distinction of having been European City of Culture and Architecture, with a rich heritage of Victorian buildings and imaginative modern designs.

Heading north, Loch Lomond was close enough to Glasgow for many of the slum dwellers of the depression years to escape the grind of dirt and poverty and breathe in the freedom of the hills. From here, and east through the beautiful countryside of the Trossachs, is Scotland's first National Park. A few hundred years ago cattle rustlers roamed here and the outlawed Rob Roy MacGregor evaded capture for years amongst the dense heather on these hillsides. The hardy Glasgow outdoor types of the 1930s slept amongst this heather while they enjoyed the scenery. They also

---

PUBLIC TRANSPORT ⓘ

Glasgow is well served by an extensive rail network and a small underground known as the Clockwork Orange. The railways are reasonably extensive in the Greater Glasgow area but further afield, particularly in the south west, rail travel varies from sparse to non-existent (Strathclyde Passenger Transport 08457 484950 or www.spt.co.uk). Details of the public bus network are available from www.stagecoachbus.com and 0141 552 4961. CalMac ferries serve the island of Arran and the Kintyre and Cowal peninsulas (information from 01475 650100 or www.calmac.co.uk).

tramped to the west of Loch Lomond to the area around Tarbert, which they named the Arrochar Alps. Here they learned the skills that would take some of them to the summits of the world's highest mountains.

The road to Argyll was constructed by Major Caufield after the Jacobite rising of 1745 and stretches of the original road still remain. Argyll is one of the oldest areas of settlement in Scotland. It was here that the Scotti first settled from Ireland and established the kingdom that is now known as Scotland. Further up that glen, earlier inhabitants left their story embedded in the valley in a series of stone monuments, astronomical sites and cemeteries.

This book is a walk through Scotland's story, from the ancient Celts, to the artistic, literary and scientific greats of the 19th and 20th centuries. It tells of the people, who lived, worked, played and died on this soil and of the land itself, challenging and majestic, undeniably beautiful and yet treacherous.

Using this Book

Information panels

An information panel for each walk shows its relative difficulty (➤ 5), the distance and total amount of ascent. An indication of the gradients you will encounter is shown by the rating 🔺🔺🔺 (no steep slopes) to 🔺🔺🔺 (several very steep slopes).

Maps

There are 30 maps, covering 40 of the walks. Some walks have a suggested option in the same area. The information panel for these walks will tell you how much extra walking is involved. On short-cut suggestions the panel will tell you the total distance if you set out from the start of the main walk. Where an option returns to the same point on the main walk, just the distance of the loop is given. Where an option leaves the main walk at one point and returns to it at another, then the distance shown is for the whole walk. The minimum time suggested is for reasonably fit walkers and doesn't allow for stops. Each walk has a suggested map. Laminated aqua3 maps are longer lasting and water resistant.

Start Points

The start of each walk is given as a six-figure grid reference prefixed by two letters indicating which 100km square of the National Grid it refers to. You'll find more information on grid references on most Ordnance Survey maps.

Dogs

We have tried to give dog owners useful advice about how dog friendly each walk is. Please respect other countryside users. Keep your dog under control, especially around livestock, and obey local bylaws and other dog control notices.

Car Parking

Many of the car parks suggested are public, but occasionally you may find you have to park on the roadside or in a lay-by. Please be considerate when you leave your car, ensuring that access roads or gates are not blocked and that other vehicles can pass safely. Remember that pub car parks are private and should not be used unless you have the owner's permission.

Walk 1

Caerlaverock Castle and the Solway Merses

A ramble taking in an ancient fortress and a National Nature Reserve.

•DISTANCE•	5¼ miles (8.4km)
•MINIMUM TIME•	2hrs 30min
•ASCENT / GRADIENT•	82ft (25m) ▲ ▲ ▲
•LEVEL OF DIFFICULTY•	🚶 🚶 🚶
•PATHS•	Country lanes, farm tracks and salt marsh, 1 stile
•LANDSCAPE•	Pastures, salt marsh, riverside and hills
•SUGGESTED MAP•	aqua3 OS Explorer 314 Solway Firth
•START / FINISH•	Grid reference: NY 051656
•DOG FRIENDLINESS•	Keep on lead while on reserve
•PARKING•	Car park at Wildfowl and Wetlands Trust Reserve
•PUBLIC TOILETS•	At Wildfowl and Wetlands Trust Reserve

BACKGROUND TO THE WALK

Against the impressive backdrop of Criffel, guarded by the wide waters of the Solway Firth, the salt marshes and the impressive medieval castle of Caerlaverock, this out-of-the-way corner of Scotland is a haven for wildlife and a treasure trove of history

A Castle Under Siege

Caerlaverock, the Castle of the Lark, was once the main gatekeeper to south west Scotland. Protected by mudflats and the shifting channels of the sea, it was vulnerable only from the landward side. During the Scottish Wars of Independence (1286–1370) it was attacked frequently. From the siege of Caerlaverock by Edward I in 1300 through to the 17th century it was continually beseiged, levelled and rebuilt. Its garrison last surrendered in 1640 after holding a Scottish army of Covenanters for over three months. Partially demolished, it crumbled to an ivy-covered ruin until restoration in the mid-20th century. Within the ruined walls of this triangular fortress, conservators continue their work on one of the finest Renaissance residences in Scotland.

Preserving the Balance

Conservation work of a different kind takes place on the merse (salt marsh) that bounds the Solway coast. Here Scottish Natural Heritage (SNH), the Wildfowl and Wetlands Trust (WWT) and the Caerlaverock Estate work at preserving the delicate balance that allows farming and wild fowling to exist alongside a National Nature Reserve.

The desolate open spaces, unchanged for centuries, echo to the cry of the wild geese in winter, the oystercatcher and heron in summer and the mating chorus of the natterjack toad in spring. But it wasn't always so. Wildfowling had seriously reduced the goose population to a few hundred in 1957, when the local landowner, the Duke of Norfolk, agreed to divide the merse into an area for controlled shooting and a wildlife sanctuary, now the National Nature Reserve. This is also one of the last places in Britain where scientists can study the natural processes of growth and erosion of salt marshes.

Walk 1

Sir Peter Scott

In 1970 the duke offered the naturalist, Sir Peter Scott, the lease of Eastpark Farm for the WWT. Here, every October, the Spitsbergen population of barnacle geese fly in from Norway to their winter quarters along the merse. The birds can be seen from specially constructed hides along roads shielded with high hedges to minimise disturbance to wildlife.

Whooper swans overwinter here too, along with the pink-footed goose, pintail, scaup, oystercatcher, knot, bar-tailed godwit, curlew and redshank. Staff at Eastpark organise a variety of events to help visitors appreciate the reserve, including birdwatching, natterjack toad and bat spotting and pond dipping. As part of the conservation process, wildfowling is permitted in winter. Barnacle geese are protected but other species are fair game. The wildfowlers are experts at recognition and the SNH wardens ensure fair play.

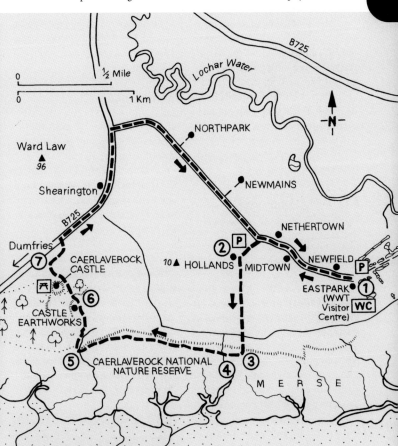

Walk 1 Directions

① Exit the car park and turn right on to a farm road. Follow this past the farms of **Newfield** and **Midtown** then turn left and go past a bungalow and some houses. Just before the farm of **Hollands** there is a waymarker pointing to a car park, on the right, and straight ahead for walks. Go straight ahead, continue to the farm steading and turn left.

② Go through a gate and on to a farm track. This stretches away into the distance and has high hedges on both sides. Continue along this track between the hedges and on, over an overgrown section, until you reach a fence. Cross this by a stile and turn right at the signpost indicating **Caerlaverock National Nature Reserve**.

③ A sign here informs visitors that regulated wildfowling (shooting) takes place between 1 September and 20 February. Follow the rough track through the grass along the edge of the merse in the direction of the arrow on the footpath waymarker post. The path can be very boggy at all times and the grass will be high in summer.

WHERE TO EAT AND DRINK ℹ

There's an excellent, newly opened family-friendly café and tea room in the visitors' centre at **Eastpark**. It is bright and spacious and serves a good range of hot food and beverages, snacks and cakes. It also houses the WWT gift and bookshop.

---

④ Cross a small wooden bridge, an electric fence covered with a piece of insulated piping and another small bridge. The path splits at several points and meanders back and forth but all the lines of the path rejoin and you'll end up at the same place which ever one you take.

⑤ Eventually a tumbledown wire and post fence will appear on the right-hand side. Follow this fence towards a wood, passing through an overgrown area and then bear right, through a gate and into a field. Walk to the left around the perimeter of this field, past some cottages, and then turn left through

---

WHILE YOU'RE THERE ℹ

The **Dumfries Museum and Camera Obscura** is housed in a former windmill and has a comprehensive collection covering the history of the region, its people and wildlife. Here you'll see fossils, stone carvings by early Christians, a range of Victoriana, some death masks, a plaster cast of the skull of Robert Burns and the first writings of J M Barrie who who lived in Dumfries for a time.

---

a gate to emerge on to a farm track, passing a sign pointing the way for **Caerlaverock Castle** and into the castle grounds.

⑥ Follow the road past the old castle, which has been excavated and has information boards to explain the ruins, and go through a wood with nature trail information boards to **Caerlaverock Castle**. There is a children's playground, a siege machine and picnic tables around the ramparts of the castle.

⑦ At the far end go through an arch and continue to the T-junction with a country lane. Turn right and continue for about a mile (1.6km) then turn right on to another lane signposted 'Wildfowl and Wetlands Reserve'. Continue on this road past the farms of **Northpark**, **Newmains** and **Nethertown** and then back to the car park at **Eastpark**.

WHAT TO LOOK FOR ℹ

While on the salt marsh and mudflats section of this walk the large hill immediately in front of you is Criffel (► Walk 3). Look out along here for **grebes** and wintering **goldeneye** and in the spring for the **black-tailed godwit** on passage. In spring and summer this area is particularly rich in **wild flowers**. You'll need to carry a field guide with you to get the most from the walk.

The Solway Shore from Carsethorn to Arbigland

Visit the birthplace of John Paul Jones, the 'father of the American Navy'.

·DISTANCE·	5½ miles (8.8km)
·MINIMUM TIME·	2hrs 30min
·ASCENT / GRADIENT·	82ft (25m) ▲▲ ▲ ▲
·LEVEL OF DIFFICULTY·	林林 林 林
·PATHS·	Rocky seashore, woodland tracks and country roads
·LANDSCAPE·	Seashore, woodland and pasture
·SUGGESTED MAP·	aqua3 OS Explorer 313 Dumfries & Dalbeattie, New Abbey
·START / FINISH·	Grid reference: NX 993598
·DOG FRIENDLINESS·	Good walk for dogs
·PARKING·	Car park by beach at Carsethorn
·PUBLIC TOILETS·	At John Paul Jones Museum

BACKGROUND TO THE WALK

The man hailed in the USA as the 'father of the American Navy' was born John Paul in a poor gardener's cottage at Arbigland, on the Solway coast in 1745.

Young Seaman

At the age of 13 John signed up as an apprentice seaman journeying to Virginia on the *Friendship of Whitehaven*. He later signed on as third mate on a slave ship, the *King George of Whitehaven*. He lasted two years and advanced to first mate before he quit in disgust with the slave trade. On his passage home he acquired his first command when the captain and mate of his vessel died of fever. As the only qualified man left, John took control and brought the ship safely home. The owners rewarded him with permanent command. He had a reputation for a fiery temper and was once charged with murder but found not guilty. In 1773 he fled the West Indies, after killing the ringleader of a mutiny, and went to Virginia where he had inherited some property. It was around this time that he changed his name to John Paul Jones.

American Naval Officer

In the lead up to the American Revolution (War of American Independence) when Congress was forming a 'Continental Navy', Jones offered his services and was commissioned as a first lieutenant on the *Alfred* in 1775. Later, as captain of the *Providence*, he advised Congress on naval regulations. In 1778, after a daring hit-and-run raid on Whitehaven, he sailed across the Solway to Kirkcudbright Bay to kidnap the Earl of Selkirk and ransom him for American captives. However the earl was not at home and the raiding party had to be content with looting the family silver.

Famous Battle

In September 1779, as commodore of a small squadron of French ships, John Paul Jones engaged his ship the *Bonhomme Richard* with the superior HMS *Serapis* and HMS *Countess of Scarborough* off Flamborough Head. After a dreadful 4-hour fight, in which Jones was injured and his ship sunk, he eventually won the battle, transferred his crew to the *Serapis* and sailed for Holland with his prisoners and booty.

John Paul Jones died in France in 1792 and his body lay in an unmarked grave for over a century. His remains were eventually taken back to the USA amid great ceremony and was finally laid to rest in the chapel crypt of the Annapolis Naval Academy in 1913.

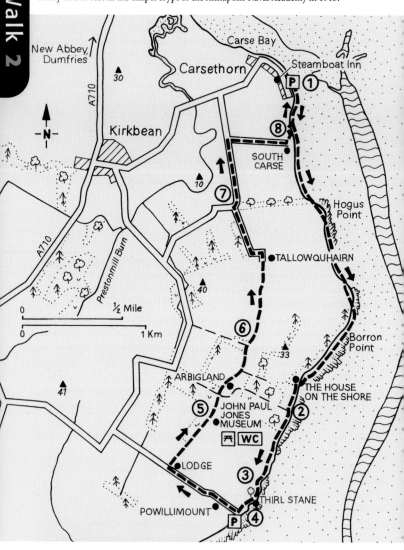

Walk 2 **Directions**

① From the car park at **Carsethorn** head down on to the beach and turn right. Continue walking along the shore for approximately 2 miles (3.2km). The beach at this point is sandy and may be strewn with driftwood, but if the tide is in you will be walking over more rocky ground.

② After you reach **The House on the Shore**, which is beside the beach on your right, the headland juts out and you should look for a track heading uphill on the right. At the top of the hill a well-defined track heads alongside a stone wall.

> ### WHERE TO EAT AND DRINK
> The **Steamboat Inn**, just opposite the car park at Carsethorn has been trading since 1813 and, while offering up-to-the-minute comforts, still retains the atmosphere of those bygone days when immigrants left here to take the steamer to Liverpool for onward transport to the colonies. A real fire, real ales and a reputation for the best food in the district makes this a natural choice for walkers and families.

③ Look for a fainter track leading off to the left, which descends steeply to arrive at the beach beside a natural rock arch called the **Thirl Stane**. You can go through the arch to the sea if the tide is in, although if the tide is out on this part of the coast, the sea will be far off in the distance.

④ Continue from here along the rocks on the pebble shore and up a grassy bank until you reach a car park. Exit the car park on to a lane. Continue on the lane past **Powillimount**. Turn right when you get to a lodge house on the right-hand side and walk along the estate road to reach the cottage birthplace of John Paul Jones.

⑤ There are picnic tables here and a fascinating small **museum**. Continue along the road past the gates to **Arbigland** on to the road signed 'No vehicular traffic'. Follow the road as it turns right and along the side of some of the Arbigland Estate buildings.

⑥ When the road turns left at a cottage, go right on to a dirt track. Follow the dirt track until it emerges on to a surfaced road next to **Tallowquhairn** to your right. Take the road away from the farm, turning sharply left around some houses, then right and continue to a T-junction.

⑦ Turn right and follow this road round to the left. Follow the long straight road as far as the right turn to **South Carse**. Go along the farm road and straight through the farm steading as far as you can go, then turn left.

> ### WHAT TO LOOK FOR
> The rocks between Hogus Point and Arbigland date from the Carboniferous era some 345 million years ago. **Fossils** in this area are well exposed and those of coral, cuttlefish, fish vertebrae, shells and tooth plates can be found. Near the beach at Powillimount look for fossilised tree ferns.

⑧ To return to the shore again, walk along a footpath passing a brightly coloured caravan and the rear of some cottages. Look out for a narrow track heading downhill to the right allowing access to the beach. Turn left and walk along the beach to the car park.

> ### WHILE YOU'RE THERE
> The Victorian **Shambellie House**, just outside the village of New Abbey, contains a unique collection of costumes and is part of the National Museums of Scotland. Most of the clothes are displayed in natural settings in a series of tableaux. In the dining room is an after dinner game of carpet bowls c1905 while two women in 1920s evening dress are playing the gramophone in the library and a 1930s bride is getting dressed in the bedroom.

Criffel and New Abbey

A 13th-century love story of the Lady Devorgilla, set forever in stone.

Walk 3

•DISTANCE•	3¾ miles (6km)
•MINIMUM TIME•	3hrs
•ASCENT / GRADIENT•	1,686ft (514m) ▲▲▲
•LEVEL OF DIFFICULTY•	🚶 🚶 🚶
•PATHS•	Forest road, rough hill and wood tracks, 1 stile
•LANDSCAPE•	Hills, tidal estuary, woods and pasture
•SUGGESTED MAP•	aqua3 OS Explorer 313 Dumfries & Dalbeattie
•START / FINISH•	Grid reference: NX 971634
•DOG FRIENDLINESS•	Keep on lead near livestock
•PARKING•	Car park at Ardwall farm
•PUBLIC TOILETS•	None on route

BACKGROUND TO THE WALK

The majestic ruins of Sweetheart Abbey dominate the village of New Abbey. Set against the backdrop of Criffel, Dumfries's highest hill, they stand as testimony to one woman's love, devotion and determination.

A Lasting Memorial

Sweetheart Abbey was founded in 1273 by Devorgilla, Lady of Galloway, as a memorial to her late husband, John Balliol, and as a last resting place for them both. When Balliol died at Barnard Castle in 1269, Devorgilla had his heart removed from his corpse, embalmed and placed in a silver mounted ivory casket which she carried everywhere with her.

Devorgilla lived long enough to see the graceful abbey rise beside the River Nith. She died in 1289 at Barnard Castle, Durham, and her body was carried to Dumfries, her last journey following that of her husband through the north of England into Scotland. She was interred at Sweetheart Abbey, next to her husband near the high altar, and the cask containing his heart was placed on her breast. Her devotion and attachment to her husband led the monks to give the abbey the name *dulce cor* or sweet heart. Within the abbey there can still be seen a, now headless, effigy of her holding the casket.

Originally the abbey was called New Abbey, to distinguish it from the nearby mother house of Dundrennan, and so the village that subsequently grew up around it took its name. At the Reformation, supported by the local population and the powerful Maxwell family, the abbot, Gilbert Brown, refused to give up the abbey. Eventually, in 1610, after two evictions and arrests, he was finally sent into exile.

The villagers had considerable affection for the abbey and, in 1779, started a fund to ensure its preservation. Now under the care of Historic Scotland, it remains one of the most impressive abbey ruins in Scotland. Although the roof has gone, the cruciform church and massive central tower, built from red Dumfriesshire sandstone, still stand.

The monks of Dundrennan, Glenluce and New Abbey were members of the Order of the Cistercians founded in 1098 at Citeaux in Burgundy. Directed by the rule of St Benedict they observed a life of poverty, chastity and obedience. In 1136, some white monks of this order travelled north from Rievaulx, in Yorkshire, to found the abbey at Melrose and six years later came to Dundrennan. At the time of Devorgilla's death, there were 11 Cistercian monasteries in Scotland.

Although they lived an austere life the Cistercians played an important part in the trading network. They were the largest producers of wool in the country, at their peak accounting for around 5 per cent of Scotland's total wool production. They provided much needed employment and helped establish towns and burghs throughout the country.

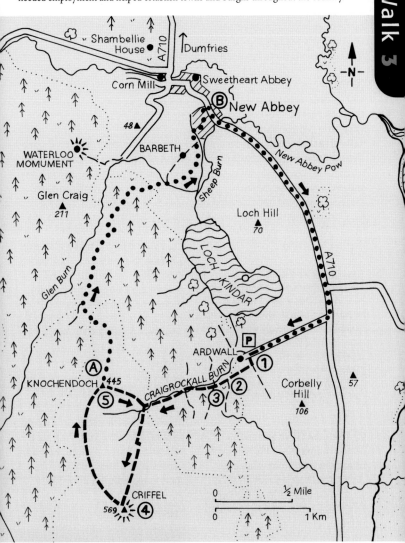

Walk 3 **Directions**

① From the car park head towards **Ardwall farm** then go through a gate on the left. Turn right after

70yds (64m) then head towards the hill on a track between dry-stone walls. When the road curves left, in front of the wood, take the rough track off to the right. (The Criffel Walk sign has fallen from its post.)

Walk 3

② Follow a well-trodden track uphill and through the trees following the course of the **Craigrockall Burn**. The path narrows in places and the ground is very uneven with several large boulders to climb over or around. Many trees have been felled here and it is not long before you emerge from the woods on to open hillside.

③ When you reach a T-junction with a forest road, keep straight ahead to pick up the trail on the other side and continue uphill. The ground can be very boggy, even in summer, and care needs to be taken. Cross another forest road and eventually reach a fence marking where the tree line used to be. Cross the stile here and veer to the left, heading towards the summit of **Criffel**.

WHERE TO EAT AND DRINK

Conveniently situated right at the entrance to Sweetheart Abbey is the **Abbey Cottage tea room** where visitors can enjoy anything from a cup of tea and a scone to snacks and light meals. Elsewhere in New Abbey its worth taking the time to check out the 19th-century, Tudor-style **Criffel Inn** with its superb selection of cask beers and over 120 malt whiskies. The atmospheric bar is also the best place to sample their excellent meals, freshly prepared using local produce.

When you've eaten your picnic and enjoyed the view (► What To Look For) head roughly north west from the cairn, then go north crossing over rough ground towards the broad ridge that runs from Criffel to the neighbouring hill of Knochendoch. When you intersect a narrow footpath turn right, head downhill on it then continue, ascending again now, to reach the summit of **Knochendoch**.

WHILE YOU'RE THERE

There's an opportunity to see how oatmeal and flour were produced at **New Abbey Corn Mill**. This classic example of a Galloway country mill is the last survivor of a once common-place industry. The fully restored, working, 18th-century mill is powered by a waterwheel and offers regular demonstrations of the miller's trade.

⑤ From the summit cairn head east and go downhill. In the summer, when the heather is particularly thick, the going can be fairly tough and you'll have to proceed slowly and with caution. Make for the fence that runs across the hill in front of you. Turn right here and follow it back to the stile. Cross the stile and retrace your steps to the bottom of the hill.

④ From the OS triangulation pillar on the summit of Criffel you will have a view into four kingdoms. Across the Solway to the south is England and the hills of the Lake District. A little to the right of that is the ancient Celtic kingdom of the Isle of Man, while the coast of Ireland is visible to the west. The ancient Scotti tribe came from Ireland and founded the kingdom of Scotland. On a good day the summit of Criffel is the best restaurant in town, provided you have remembered to pack the food.

WHAT TO LOOK FOR

From the summit of Criffel look east towards Caerlaverock Castle on the opposite bank of the River Nith. Beyond that you will be able to see the massive cooling towers of **Chapelcross** nuclear power station standing out like a sore thumb enclosed in a patchwork of lush rolling pastures, marked out by ancient dry-stone walls.

Walk 4

Knochendoch to New Abbey

It's downhill most of the way to Devorgilla's Sweetheart Abbey.
See map and information panel for Walk 3

•DISTANCE•	7¾ miles (12.5km)
•MINIMUM TIME•	6hrs
•ASCENT / GRADIENT•	1,768ft (539m) ▲▲ ▲ ▲
•LEVEL OF DIFFICULTY•	🚶🚶 🚶🚶 🚶

Walk 4 Directions
(Walk 3 option)

From the summit of **Knochendoch** (Point Ⓐ) head roughly north and pick up a rough path heading downhill with a wall on the left. Continue to descend following the wall to a corner with a fence and cross a stile on the left. Continue downhill from here with the wall on your right. Look up, ahead and to the left for a tower-like building on top of **Waterloo Hill**. This monument commemorates the Battle of Waterloo.

Access to the monument from New Abbey is by an easy walk on the minor road to Mid Glen and then by footpath up the hill. Some 49ft (15m) high, the monument has a winding stone staircase inside, leading to the top where you can enjoy views of the village, Dumfries, Caerlaverock and Shambellie House museum. According to the inscription it was built in 1816 to 'record the valour of those British, Belgian and Prussian soldiers who under Wellington and Blutcher on the 18th of June 1815 gained the victory at Waterloo by which French tyranny was overthrown and peace restored to the world.'

This is fairly typical of the many Waterloo monuments built at the time and conveys some impression of the impact the Napoleonic Wars had on the area.

Continue carefully on the descending path as the ground is very boggy until you enter a larch forest where the surface becomes firmer. Shortly clear the forest and the path ends at a junction with a forest road. Turn right, follow the road, crossing a stile, a gate and a bridge. Do not go through the gate at the end of the bridge but turn right and continue on the road.

Look out on the grass verges and ditches by the roadside for a variety of wild flowers including the heath spotted orchid, a profusion of lesser celandine, foxgloves, red campion and a variety of ferns.

From here go through another four gates and, shortly after the last one, go right when the path forks to join the drive to **Barbeth farm**. Go through a set of gates at the end of the road to arrive in **New Abbey** (Point Ⓑ). Follow this road through the village to the **A710** then turn right. Walk for about 2 miles (3.2km) to the turn off to **Ardwall farm** on the right. Turn up here and return to the car park.

A Dumfries Town Trail

In the footsteps of Burns and Barrie around the birthplace of Peter Pan.

•DISTANCE•	5½ miles (8.8km)
•MINIMUM TIME•	2hrs
•ASCENT / GRADIENT•	Negligible
•LEVEL OF DIFFICULTY•	🚶🚶 🚶 🚶
•PATHS•	Pavements
•LANDSCAPE•	Town streets and river bank
•SUGGESTED MAP•	aqua3 OS Explorer 313 Dumfries & Dalbeattie, New Abbey
•START / FINISH•	Grid reference: NX 976765
•DOG FRIENDLINESS•	Keep on lead
•PARKING•	Dumfries Station
•PUBLIC TOILETS•	Dumfries Station

Walk 5 Directions

With the railway station behind you turn left. Leave the car park, turn left at the **Waverley Hotel** and go over the railway bridge. Go over a roundabout and then turn left when you reach **Victoria Terrace**, a handsome row of substantial houses with their gardens across the road. Barrie lived at No 6, as an engraving on the wall testifies: 'Sir James Mathew Barrie BART OM 1860–1937, Scottish novelist and dramatist. J M Barrie lived in this house, the home of his brother, while a scholar at Dumfries Academy from 1873 to 1878. He regarded his stay in Dumfries as among his happiest days. In 1924 he was made a freeman of Dumfries the town where Peter Pan was born.'

Retrace your steps to the road and turn right. Go back across the roundabout and continue past the **Waverley Hotel**, the traffic-lights and the County Buildings until you come to **Shakespeare Street** on your left. Cross the road and turn

into it. Pass the **Theatre Royal**, where Burns was a patron, and turn left into **Burns Street**.

> **WHERE TO EAT AND DRINK**
>
> The **Doonhamer**, just along from Dumfries Academy offers a fascinating mixture of Scottish traditional cooking and Italian cuisine. Run by the Rinaldi family this is one of the most popular eating places in Dumfries, where you can get anything from a traditional breakfast to a plate of mince and tatties or one of their pasta creations. Children welcome.

The street winds uphill, passing **Burns House** on the left, then reaches a junction. Turn left and head across a road to **St Michaels Church** and visit the Burns Mausoleum in the churchyard. Retrace your footsteps to the top of **Burns Street** and continue down **Nith Place**. Cross the road at the bottom in front of the **Loreburn Centre** and turn into the pedestrian area of the **High Street**.

Look out for the sign and entrance close of the **Globe Inn**, to the right, opposite Marks and Spencer, and go in to visit Burns' favourite haunt. Here he would regularly hold court of an evening and if he had a few too many would often stay over night in the room upstairs. You can try his personal chair for size, but be warned that anyone who sits here who can't recite some of the bard's work must stand the rest of the company a drink. In the upstairs bedroom Burns scratched a few verses of poetry on the window pane and they can still be seen.

> **WHAT TO LOOK FOR** ⓘ
> While crossing the 15th-century Devorgilla's Bridge have a look at the **Old Bridge House** built of red sandstone into the fabric of the bridge. This dates from 1660 and is the oldest house in Dumfries. It is now a museum of everyday life and within is a Victorian nursery, kitchens recreated from the 1850s and 1900s and a very scary looking early dentists surgery.

Come back through the close and turn right. Head past the fountain in the direction of the Mid Steeple and turn left down **Bank Street**. Near the bottom of the street look up on the right for a couple of plaques, which identify the building Burns and his family moved to in 1791 when they vacated Ellisland Farm. Here, over 18 months, he wrote over 60 songs including the poignant love song *Ae Fond Kiss*.

Continue to the **Whitesands** and cross the road to the banks of the **Nith**. Turn left and walk beside the river to the suspension bridge. Turn right and cross the bridge, head up **Suspension Brae** and turn right on to **Troqueer Road**. Head uphill to the **Dumfries Museum and Camera Obscura**, housed in an old windmill. Here, if you ask, you can see the earliest known example of

Barrie's writing, *Rekollections of a Skoolmaster*, which was published in a school magazine produced by one of Barrie's childhood friends.

Continue past the museum and, at the end of a block of sandstone buildings on your right, turn right and go down some steps to reach the **Robert Burns Centre**. Exit the Burns Centre, and turn right along the riverside to the ancient **Devorgilla's Bridge**, which you cross to reach the **Whitesands** again. Cross the road and make your way up **Friars Vennel**. Turn left at the top, pass Burns Statue and cross the road to Greyfriars church. Go to the left of the church along **Castle Street** and turn right at the crossroads.

Continue to the last house on the left, opposite the entrance to **Dumfries Academy**. This is **Moat Brae** the former home of Barrie's friend Wellwood (Wed) Anderson. It was here that the tale of *Peter Pan* had its origins as Barrie and his friends played pirates in the garden.

From here go along **Irvine Street**, turn left at the junction and go along the front of **Dumfries Academy** where Barrie went to school. At the second set of traffic-lights turn right into **Lovers Walk** to return to the railway station.

> **WHILE YOU'RE THERE** ⓘ
> Visit **Burns House** which you pass on the walk. This is where the poet finally settled in Dumfries and it is preserved much the way it was when he lived here. The curator is a knowledgeable and friendly man who can tell you anything you need to know about Burns, show you the bed he died in and the desk where he copied down the words of *Auld Lang Syne*.

Walk 6

The Glenkiln Outdoor Sculptures

Discover the works of Henry Moore, Epstein and Rodin in a unique countryside setting.

•DISTANCE•	4 miles (6.4km)
•MINIMUM TIME•	2hrs 30min
•ASCENT / GRADIENT•	312ft (95m)
•LEVEL OF DIFFICULTY•	
•PATHS•	Country roads, farm tracks, open hillside
•LANDSCAPE•	Sculptures, hills, woodland and reservoir
•SUGGESTED MAP•	aqua3 OS Explorer 321 Nithsdale & Dumfries
•START / FINISH•	Grid reference: NX 839784
•DOG FRIENDLINESS•	Keep on lead on farmland particularly at lambing time
•PARKING•	Car park in front of statue of John the Baptist
•PUBLIC TOILETS•	None on route or near by

BACKGROUND TO THE WALK

During the mid-1950s Tony Keswick, a Dumfriesshire landowner with a penchant for sculpture, acquired a copy of August Rodin's *John the Baptist* from the Musée Rodin in Paris. Keswick did not hide it away in a darkened vault or even in a gallery. It stands today, as it always has, in open countryside, atop a hillock, its outstretched arm beckoning across the water of Glenkiln Reservoir.

An Amazing Collection
Keswick was given the hill farm of Glenkiln by his father in 1924 as a 21st birthday present but he rarely visited it until the 1950s. That first Rodin was the start of an amazing collection of art in the landscape at Glenkiln. On a visit to the studio of sculptor Henry Moore, he immediately recognised that Moore's *Standing Figure* would be ideal placed on a large flat boulder that stood by the roadside near the farm. This was followed by Moore's *King and Queen*. Of the six casts made, the Glenkiln piece is the only one in a private collection. Keswick tried a number of sites around his land before placing it on a hillside overlooking the reservoir. They look out serenely over their domain, separate from, yet part of the landscape that surrounds them.

Hard Times
Epstein's *Visitation* is in the collection of the Tate Gallery in London. Keswick obtained Epstein's own copy purely by chance. He was with the artist when a group of workmen arrived to cart the work off to melt it down. Epstein, although famous, was so hard up that he was selling some of his work for scrap to pay the foundry bill for a bust of Winston Churchill he was working on. Keswick was appalled and promptly bought the statue.

The statue depicts the Virgin Mary with folded hands, head slightly bowed and an expression of utmost serenity on her face. She's located a bit off the beaten track and surrounded by Scots pine within the tumbledown walls of a long abandoned sheep fold. To stumble, seemingly almost by accident, on this figure, particularly on a slightly dark and misty winter's day, when the sheep have gathered around her, is one of the magical moments of Glenkiln.

Glenkiln has been a popular attraction since Tony Keswick placed his first sculpture out of doors. He positively encouraged people to come and see the collection and today it remains as a tribute not just to the work of the artists but to the memory of a remarkable man who saw sculpture as a complement to nature.

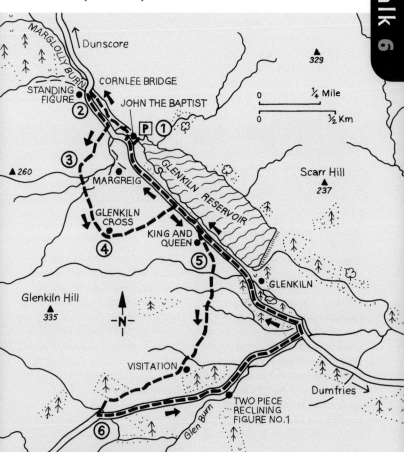

Walk 6 Directions

① From the car park in front of the statue *John the Baptist* return to the main road and turn right. Cross a cattle grid then turn right and go past the statue to the **Marglolly Burn**. Turn left and walk along the bank towards **Cornlee Bridge**. Just before the bridge turn left and head

back to the road. Henry Moore's *Standing Figure* is before you at the junction with a farm road.

② Turn left and head back along the main road. Just before the entrance to **Margreig farm** on the right is a muddy track running across the field to a gate in the dry-stone wall. Head up and through the gate then keep straight ahead,

Walk 6

uphill and towards a telephone pole. At the pole veer left and follow the track uphill. The **Glenkiln Cross** should now be visible in front of you.

③ There are several footpaths and tracks available. Take the one that is closest to a large tree in front of you. Cross a burn at the tree then take the path that skirts to the left of it. Veer right and head for the high ground. Once the cross comes into view again head directly towards it.

> **WHILE YOU'RE THERE** ⓘ
>
> Enjoy a visit to **Ellisland** the Dumfriesshire farm where Robert Burns wrote *Tam O' Shanter*. Situated on the A76, a few miles north of Dumfries, this is where Burns came with his bride, Jean Armour, to start a new life as a farmer. Unfortunately the land was poor, the venture failed and the poet moved to Dumfries and life as an exciseman.

④ From the cross turn to face **Glenkiln Reservoir** then head downhill towards a telephone pole. Go through a gate in the fence at the bottom of the hill and turn right on to the road. A short distance along here a farm track leads uphill to the right. Go through a gate and on to it. To your right on the hillside is Henry Moore's *King and Queen*.

> **WHAT TO LOOK FOR** ⓘ
>
> It's easy to miss, but just after going through the gate on the farm track past the *King and Queen*, look out for a small block of Dumfriesshire sandstone on the right. It's weathered and a bit faded but you can still make out the inscription. On one side is 'Glenkiln' and on the other 'Henry Moore 1898–1986'. This was Tony Keswick's personal **memorial** to his favourite sculptor.

> **WHERE TO EAT AND DRINK** ⓘ
>
> This is a fairly remote spot and ideal for a picnic. Alternatives include the **George Hotel** in the picturesque village of Dunscore about 6 miles (9.7km) away or the **Craigdarroch Arms** in the even more picturesque village of Moniaive beyond that. Both are friendly family-run establishments providing good wholesome food in a traditional country bar setting.

⑤ Continue on this track. Go through a gate, pass a small wooded area on your right and then bare hillside until you spot a small stand of Scots pine on the left. Leave the road at this point and continue to the trees and Epstein's *Visitation*. Return to the road and continue to the end where you go through a gate, over a bridge then turn left on to the road.

⑥ Go downhill on this road for ½ mile (800m), crossing a cattle grid. Just before the end of the conifer plantation on the left, look out for Moore's *Two Piece Reclining Figure No 1* on your right. Follow the road all the way downhill from here, turn left at the junction and continue on this road until you reach the car park.

The Last Turning in Moniaive

The village that inspired the 19th-century school of artists known as the Glasgow Boys.

•DISTANCE•	5 miles (8km)
•MINIMUM TIME•	3hrs
•ASCENT / GRADIENT•	295ft (90m) ▲▲▲
•LEVEL OF DIFFICULTY•	🚶🚶🚶
•PATHS•	Dirt roads, hill tracks, forest road and country lane
•LANDSCAPE•	Hills and woodland
•SUGGESTED MAP•	aqua3 OS Explorers 321 Nithsdale & Dumfries, Thornhill; 328 Sanquhar & New Cumnock, Muirkirk
•START / FINISH•	Grid reference: NX 780910 (on Explorer 328)
•DOG FRIENDLINESS•	Keep on lead near livestock
•PARKING•	Moniaive village car park
•PUBLIC TOILETS•	Ayr Street, passed on walk

BACKGROUND TO THE WALK

Moniaive is one of Scotland's most picturesque villages. Situated at a crossroads where the waters of three glens meet, it has a natural attraction for artists. James Paterson came here in the summer of 1879, the first of several summer painting visits. When he married in 1884 he decided to settle in Moniaive and moved into Kilneis on the outskirts of the village. Originally a small stone cottage, Paterson's father commissioned the architect John James Burnet to enlarge it as a wedding present to his son and his bride.

A Rebellious Bunch

Paterson was born in Glasgow in 1854 to a prosperous middle class family of cotton and muslin manufacturers. He persuaded his father to make him a small allowance to enable him to study art in Paris. Courting controversy, he became part of the group of painters known as the Glasgow Boys, which included W Y Macgregor, E A Walton and James Guthrie, who would meet at life classes in Macgregor's Glasgow studio. They were a rebellious bunch and detested the moribund traditions of the Royal Scottish Academy (RSA). Influenced by the realism of contemporary French painters, they successfully exhibited in London and throughout Europe while being ignored by the Scottish establishment. In later life their painting became more conservative and Paterson was finally elected to the RSA and became its librarian and secretary.

Landscape Painter

Much of Paterson's finest work was completed in Moniaive. A dedicated landscape painter, he had a wooden studio built on the banks of Craigdarroch Water. Today his watercolours and oils can be found in galleries throughout the world but his most famous work hangs in Glasgow's Kelvingrove Museum and Art Gallery. *The Last Turning* shows a woman in black walking along a country lane. To her left is the water of a mill pond and across it the spire of the clock tower on the schoolmaster's house. The pond is long gone, replaced by a century's growth of trees, but everything else remains the same and in winter it is still possible to glimpse the tower through the trees.

From 1897 Paterson had a studio in Edinburgh and lived for only part of the year in Moniaive. By 1906 he had moved his family permanently to the capital and finally sold Kilneis in 1917. He died in Edinburgh in 1932 but his son, Hamish Constable Paterson, himself an artist, returned to live in Moniaive in 1953. Another Paterson artist, Ann Paterson Wallace opened the James Paterson Museum in the village in the 1990s. With her collection of Paterson memorabilia and Paterson's own photographs, she has created a lasting memorial to her grandfather and a valuable resource for anyone wanting to study the art of the Glasgow Boys.

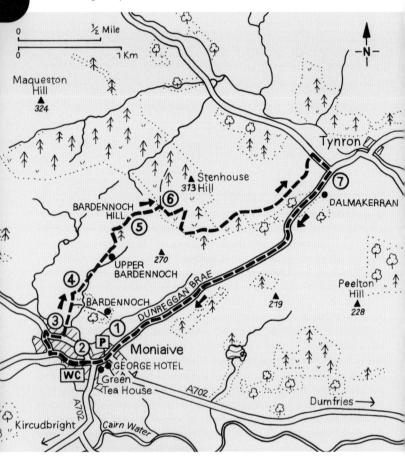

Walk 7 Directions

① Exit the car park and turn right. At a nearby T-junction turn right and go over the pedestrian bridge, beside a garage, to enter Moniaive **High Street** at the **George Hotel**. Walk along the High Street to the **Market Cross of Moniaive**, pass it then turn left and cross the road. Turn right at the other side and head up **Ayr Street,** passing the public toilets.

② The imposing building on the right with the clock tower is the former village schoolmaster's house. Continue up Ayr Street passing a park on the right and some wooden garages on the left. Take the next right on to a narrow lane. Continue to the end of the lane and, at a T-junction turn right.

③ Pass a modern bungalow on the left, then a field, then turn left on to a dirt road at the end of the field. Cross a bridge and continue up the road to **Bardennoch**. When the road curves right to enter the grounds of the house, go straight on and follow the road, which goes up the side of the wood and uphill.

④ At the end of the woodland section go through a gate and continue uphill on the road. Cross a fence and then at the top, near the ruin of **Upper Bardennoch**, go through another gate. From here continue to climb towards a stand of Scots pine, circle them keeping them on your right and continue to the summit of **Bardennoch Hill**.

⑤ From the summit keep going in the same direction towards some woodland. A wall should be running beside you to the right. Head slightly downhill to come to the corner where this wall meets one running in front of the woodland. Cross the wall and go on to a forest road.

⑥ Turn right and follow this road downhill through several gates until it goes through a final gate, at a T-junction with a country lane, where you turn right. At the next T-junction the left turn will soon take you to the hamlet of **Tynron** which is worth visiting. Otherwise turn right again.

WHILE YOU'RE THERE 🛈
Visit **Kircudbright**, an ancient town on the Solway coast west of Dumfries. The light in this part of the world is unique and has always held a fascination for artists. E A Hornel, another of the Glasgow Boys, painted here and eventually set up home in the large Georgian Broughton House. It is now a museum in the care of the National Trust for Scotland and is pretty much as Hornel left it.

⑦ Follow this road past **Dalmakerran farm** then uphill and through a hazel wood. Continue uphill passing a stone cottage on the right then, further along, another house. The road starts to go downhill again on to **Dunreggan Brae**. At the bottom of the hill re-enter **Moniaive** and turn right into the car park.

WHAT TO LOOK FOR 🛈
The lane that runs between Ayr Street and North Street is where James Patterson painted his best-known work *The Last Turning*. When you reach the stone garage turn around and look back the way you came. To the right, 100 years ago, there was a mill pond instead of trees when the unknown 'woman in black', seen in the painting, was walking along the lane.

WHERE TO EAT AND DRINK 🛈
The **Green Tea House** in Chapel Street welcomes children and serves a wonderful selection of hot meals and snacks, all made from organic ingredients by Catherine Braid – the Organic Country Cook. Try the delicious soups with freshly baked bread, bacon baps with brie, pasta dishes or some of the awesome sweet and sticky things washed down with tea or coffee from a cup the size of a soup bowl.

Wanlockhead: Scotland's Highest Village

Discover the secrets of lead and gold mining in 'God's Treasure House'.

•DISTANCE•	3¾ miles (6km)
•MINIMUM TIME•	3hrs
•ASCENT / GRADIENT•	525ft (160m) ▲▲▲
•LEVEL OF DIFFICULTY•	🚶🚶 🚶
•PATHS•	Footpaths, hill tracks, hillside and old railway lines, 1 stile
•LANDSCAPE•	Hills, mining relics and village
•SUGGESTED MAP•	aqua3 OS Explorer 329 Lowther Hills, Sanquhar & Leadhills
•START / FINISH•	Grid reference: NX 873129
•DOG FRIENDLINESS•	Keep on lead near livestock
•PARKING•	Museum of Lead Mining car park
•PUBLIC TOILETS•	At car park

BACKGROUND TO THE WALK

A unique combination of changing pressures within the earth's crust several million years ago, led to the formation of rich mineral veins in this part of the Southern Uplands. Everything from gold to zinc and copper has been found locally, but it was the rich deposits of lead that resulted in the establishment of Scotland's highest village. By the 17th century a permanent, if primitive, settlement was established. Accommodation consisted of one-room cottages with often as many as eight people living in them. They cooked over the open fire in the middle of the room and smoke was vented through a hole in the roof.

By the late 19th century, when lead mining was at its peak, some 850 people lived here in much improved cottages. These cottages were bigger, with an attic room and a proper cooking range. In 1871 the miners founded a co-operative society, bought all their supplies there and received a share of the profits. Amazingly this continued until 1971.

A Thriving Community

The miners valued the little leisure time they had and were very active in forming local clubs and societies. There were curling, bowling and quoiting clubs, a drama group and even a silver band. The Library, the second oldest subscription library in Europe, was founded in 1756 by the minister and a small group of villagers. Wanlockhead fared better than most libraries with a donation of books from the local landowner the Duke of Buccleuch. Buccleuch also allowed the miners the use of land to keep cattle and grow vegetables and, in 1842, he funded the building of a new school and the salary of the teacher.

The miners' children learned to read, write and count and could also take lessons in Latin and Greek. A government inspector visiting in 1842 was so impressed by the standard of learning he concluded that '…the children of the poor labourers of Wanlockhead are under as good, or perhaps better system of intellectual culture than even the middle class children of South Britain generally.'

As the price of lead slumped, and mines became exhausted, the miners gradually drifted away. The last of the mines, Glencrieff, closed in 1934 and the village went into

Walk

8

decline until only 30 people remained. In the 1960s the local authority offered to re-house them elsewhere but they resolutely refused to leave. Thanks to their determination, an influx of new blood, renovation of houses and the opening of the Museum of Lead Mining, Wanlockhead has survived as a community into the 21st century. But it almost vanished, like countless other mining villages, which are now just names on the map, a few ruins, fading memories, old photographs and tales.

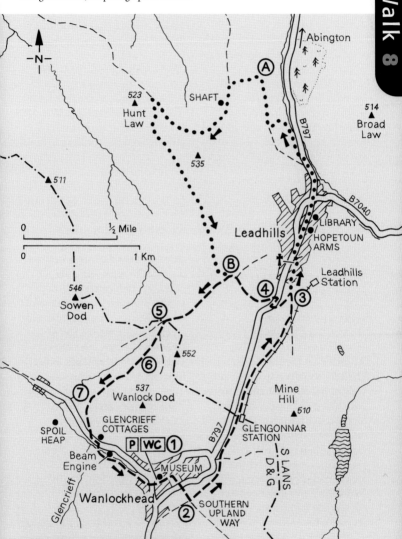

Walk 8 Directions

① With the **museum** to your back turn left and join the **Southern Upland Way**. Head uphill on steps

then, at the top, cross to a stone building with a large white door. Turn right on to a rough road, cross the main road and take the public footpath to **Enterkine Pass**. Follow this to the front of a white house.

Walk 8

② Turn left on to an old railway. Follow this, cross a road then go through a long cutting to reach a fence. Go over a stile to **Glengonnar Station** then follow the narrow path that runs along the left side of the railway tracks from here.

③ Eventually the path runs on to a rough road and in the distance you will see two terraced houses. At the point where the telephone wires intersect the road turn left at the pole on the left-hand side and follow the line of the fence down to some sheep pens. Turn right at the end of the pens and walk out to the main road.

WHERE TO EAT AND DRINK ⓘ
The **café/tea room** attached to the museum is geared towards families and has a splendid menu of light meals, sandwiches, snacks and delicious hot soup. It's a light and airy place conveniently situated where the walk begins and ends. Occasionally in the summer local musicians play traditional music here.

④ Turn right then almost immediately left on to a hill road. Walk uphill on this until the road bears sharp right and a dirt track forks off to the left (this is Point ⒷΒ on Walk 9). Turn left on to the track and keep on it until you reach a gate. Cross over then veer left on to a faint track. Follow the track downhill to the point where it comes close to the corner of a fence on your left.

⑤ Cross the fence and go straight ahead on a very faint track picking your way through the heather. Eventually, as the track begins to look more like a recognisable path, you will reach a fork. Go to the right here and cross the flank of the hill passing through some disused tips.

⑥ The path at this point is little more than a series of sheep tracks and may disappear altogether but that is not a problem. Ahead of you is a large conical spoil heap and, provided you keep heading towards it, you know you will be going in the right direction.

⑦ Towards the end of the hill the track heads left, starts to make its way downhill, then passes behind a row of cottages. Veer right, downhill, after the cottages to join the road. Turn left and continue past **Glencrieff cottages** then turn right, leaving the road and heading downhill again. Cross a bridge and climb up on to the **Southern Upland Way**. Turn left along it and follow this route back to the car park.

WHAT TO LOOK FOR ⓘ
The Wanlockhead **beam engine** was used in the 19th century to drain the Straitsteps mine. It worked by using an ingenious arrangement that filled a bucket at one end with water, thus pulling the beam end down and lifting the piston at the other end to expel the water from the mine.

WHILE YOU'RE THERE ⓘ
A visit to the **Museum of Lead Mining** before you start will greatly enhance your understanding of the area and your enjoyment of the walk. The entire history of gold and lead mining in this area is covered and the admission fee includes a visit to a former miners' cottage and a trip into one of the mines (wear warm clothing). During the summer there are gold panning demonstrations and courses. The museum is open from April to October, daily.

Leadhills Library

In the footsteps of some very literate gold and lead miners.
See map and information panel for Walk 8

•DISTANCE•	7¼ miles (11.7km)
•MINIMUM TIME•	6hrs
•ASCENT / GRADIENT•	755ft (230m) ▲▲▲
•LEVEL OF DIFFICULTY•	🚶🚶🚶

Walk 9 Directions (Walk 8 option)

At Point ③ on Walk 8, follow the north track towards **Leadhills**, passing a terrace of two houses on the right, then a short row of cottages before the track terminates at a junction with a narrow road. Turn left and walk downhill towards Leadhills church. At the junction with the **Main Street** turn right. Leadhills is the second highest village in Scotland after Wanlockhead and exists for the same reason. Rich in minerals it had always been attractive to prospectors. Gold was once found in abundance around here and was used in the Scottish crown, the oldest royal crown in Europe.

Pass the **Hopetoun Arms** hotel and then the **Leadhills Library**, the first public subscription library in Europe. In the churchyard is the grave of John Taylor, who lived to the age 137. An obelisk in front of his grave commemorates William Symington an early pioneer of steam navigation. Continue along the Main Street, go through a crossroads then pass a turning on the left on to a dirt road just before a clump of trees. After the trees are some cottages and then a rough road. Turn left on to this rough road, pass a water treatment works and continue to a gate in front of some spoil heaps. Turn right, before the gate, and follow a faint track beside the fence. Climb over a wooden section of fencing, then an old gate and strike uphill at an angle of 45 degrees.

Although the sheep tracks here are faint or non-existent you will eventually intersect a prominent cut in the hillside, Point Ⓐ. Drop into the cut, turn left and head uphill. At the end of the cut keep going to intersect a hill road. All around this part of the landscape you can see the spoil heaps, quarries and disused mine shafts left by the defunct lead mining industry and now a source of great interest for industrial archaeologists.

Turn left and follow the road as it curves right and uphill. On the right is a disused shaft and beyond it an old mine. At a fork in the road go left, then through a gate and head downhill looking for the two huge golf ball radars on Lowther Hill ahead and to the left. Go through the next gate, shortly afterwards the road turns sharp left. From the bend another road branches off to the right (Point Ⓑ).

The Battle of Glentrool

To the site of a battle that was a turning point in the Wars of Independence.

•DISTANCE•	5 miles (8km)
•MINIMUM TIME•	2hrs
•ASCENT / GRADIENT•	151ft (46m) ▲ ▲ ▲
•LEVEL OF DIFFICULTY•	🚶 🚶 🚶
•PATHS•	Forest trails, metalled roads, 1 stile
•LANDSCAPE•	Hillside, loch and woodland
•SUGGESTED MAP•	aqua3 OS Explorer 318 Galloway Forest Park North
•START / FINISH•	Grid reference: NX 396791
•DOG FRIENDLINESS•	Dogs should be kept on lead when near livestock
•PARKING•	Near entrance to Caldons Campsite
•PUBLIC TOILETS•	Caldons Campsite or Bruce's Stone car park to east

Walk 10 Directions

Leave the car park and follow the waymarks for the Loch Trool Trail. Cross the bridge over the **Water of Trool** to enter **Caldons Campsite** then turn left on to a path along the banks of the river. Cross another bridge and go past toilet blocks.

This was an area of wild, inhospitable countryside in the early 14th century – ideal for waging a guerrilla war particularly if the leader of the guerillas had a familiarity with the landscape that his opposition lacked. Robert the Bruce, the Scots commander was the grandson of one of several rivals with a claim to the Scottish throne.

> ### WHERE TO EAT AND DRINK ⓘ
> Eating places are few and far between but there is no place better for a picnic and you'll find lots of suitable spots on the walk. The nearest tea room is on the road to Glentrool at the **Stroan Bridge visitors' centre**. With friendly staff serving a variety of snacks, light meals and hot soup, it's a grand place to stop.

When the country was left without a monarch, following the death of the Maid of Norway in 1290, the Guardians of Scotland made the mistake of asking Edward I of England to settle the succession.

Edward, after a year of deliberation, decided in favour of John Balliol. Known to the Scots as Toom Tabard, or empty jacket, Balliol reigned for a mere four years before he was ritually humiliated by Edward at Montrose and forced to abdicate. Edward then claimed himself overlord of Scotland and imposed direct rule. Some of the nobility accepted Edward's rule, while others covertly backed the resistance. Many were constantly changing sides, always looking for the best political advantage. The Scottish Wars of Independence (1286–1370) were as much a civil war between rival families as a means to overthrow an oppressor.

Follow the waymarked trail through a picnic area, across a green bridge then head right across a grassy area to pick up the trail heading uphill into the forest. Go through a clearing and a kissing gate then re-enter woodland.

In 1306 Robert the Bruce murdered John, the Red Comyn, one of the other contenders for the throne, before the altar in Greyfriars church in Dumfries. Immediately going on the offensive he attacked English forces throughout the land. Crowned King of Scots at Scone on 25 March, he was then forced to flee to Rathlin Island off the Antrim coast after a series of defeats. Here, as legend would have it, Robert the Bruce shared accommodation in a cave with a spider. Whether he was inspired by the efforts of the spider or whether he spent his time planning a counter offensive is not really known. In any case he was back in Scotland by the spring of 1307 for what would be a decisive battle at Glentrool.

WHILE YOU'RE THERE ⓘ
Bladnoch Distillery near Wigtown is Scotland's most southerly whisky distillery and has a long standing reputation for producing one of the country's finest single malts. As well as distilling the amber nectar, Bladnoch also has a visitor centre telling the history of distilling and offering tours of the production process.

Continuing along the well-trodden path on the southern side of **Loch Trool** you are taking the route that the vastly superior English forces followed nearly seven centuries ago in pursuit of some Scottish rebels. Commanded by Lord Clifford and Aymer de Valence, the 1,500-strong unit was forced to dismount and eventually form a column a mile (1.6km) long. When you reach the interpretation board you are at the spot where Bruce sprung his well-planned ambush. Here, the few

Scots the English had been pursuing turned to block the path. Bruce had mustered the remainder of his 300 men on the slopes above and on his signal they hurled massive boulders down on the enemy below. It was a total rout from which the English commanders only just escaped.

Continue on the path leaving the woodland and head downhill and to the left. Cross a stile and then a footbridge to reach the Southern Upland Way and turn left. Go through two gates and over a wooden bridge and eventually reach the bridge over the **Buchan Burn**. Near here a track branches off to the left and uphill to reach **Bruce's Stone**, which was raised to commemorate the Scottish victory. It also happens to be one of the finest views in Scotland.

Glentrool was a significant turning point in Bruce's fortunes. From here he launched a series of guerrilla raids harrying the English forces and marched north into Ayrshire, where he again defeated de Valance at the Battle of Loudoun Hill. From then on Bruce's army fought on to that final decisive victory at Bannockburn, near Stirling in 1314.

Despite Bannockburn it was another 14 years, until the signing of the Treaty of Edinburgh, before England recognised an independent Scotland. Bruce died the following year and was buried at Dumfermline Abbey.

From Bruce's Stone follow the footpath to a narrow road, head through the car park and continue until you reach a waymark on the left leading to a forest trail, which returns to the start.

Cycling on the Merrick

Follow in the cycle tracks of Davie Bell, the original mountain biker.

•DISTANCE•	9 miles (14.5km)
•MINIMUM TIME•	5hrs
•ASCENT / GRADIENT•	2,339ft (713m) ▲▲▲
•LEVEL OF DIFFICULTY•	🚶 🚶 🚶
•PATHS•	Hill tracks, section to Loch Enoch can be very boggy, 1 stile
•LANDSCAPE•	Hills, lochs and trees
•SUGGESTED MAP•	aqua3 OS Explorer 318 Galloway Forest North
•START / FINISH•	Grid reference: NX 415804
•DOG FRIENDLINESS•	Keep on lead at lambing time and near stock
•PARKING•	Bruce's Stone car park
•PUBLIC TOILETS•	At car park

BACKGROUND TO THE WALK

A 1940s photograph shows a group of young men gathered round the cairn at the summit of the Merrick, south west Scotland's highest mountain. Nothing unusual there, except for the fact that they all have bicycles. It's an amazing record of the successful outcome of a challenge from a newspaper editor and a tribute to one of Ayrshire's cycling pioneers.

The Highwayman

David E T Bell (1907–65) was born and educated in Dumfries, then he moved to Ayr where he worked as a gardener. Health and fitness were his passions and when he was introduced to cycling he saw it as a means to achieve both. But Davie Bell was much more than a sportsman. He was a keen local historian and an outdoor man with an eye for nature. He had a wonderfully descriptive writing style, which ensured that thousands followed his adventures as 'The Highwayman' in his weekly column in the *Ayrshire Post*.

One week the *Post* published a letter from a reader who had gone to the summit of Merrick on a pony. He closed his correspondence with the challenge, 'It only remains for someone to make the ascent on a bicycle.' The Highwayman rose to the bait and, with four friends, set off through the mist covered Minnoch Valley heading for Merrick. Riding and walking, sometimes using a sling to carry their bikes, they progressed slowly up the hill, some of them collapsing and gasping for breath, while Davie's pal, Harry Fairbairn kept up a constant monologue, 'Jings this is smashing. I never saw anything like this.' Eventually they reached the summit and took a photograph to record the feat. Then followed the descent of the sloping ridge of the Neive of the Spit to Ben Yellery 'one hectic mile of crashing and bumping that smashed my back mudguard.' From Ben Yellery they covered another 2,000ft (610m) at a slower pace to finally descend through granite boulders to Loch Trool.

Davie Bell continued with his passion for 'rough stuff' for the rest of his life, making journeys to remote bothies like Back Hill of Bush or hauling his bike to the summit of the rocky island of Ailsa Craig in the Firth of Clyde. On each journey he took his readers with him, producing a weekly column for 30 years. When he died in 1965 subscriptions poured in from friends and admirers and a memorial cairn was erected at Rowantree Toll on the Straiton to Newton Stewart road.

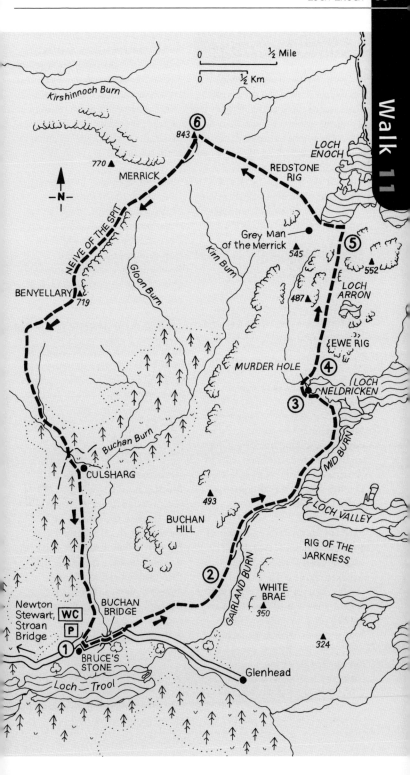

Walk 11

Walk 11 Directions

① From the car park at **Bruce's Stone** head east along the narrow road, across the **Buchan Bridge**. Continue a short distance then turn left and go uphill to cross a stile. Follow the path along the wall, then veer right and head uphill to rejoin the wall. Go through a gate and turn right on to a path. Follow this up the valley of the **Gairland Burn** with **Buchan Hill** on your left.

WHAT TO LOOK FOR ⓘ
From the corner of Loch Enoch come back a little way to the south west, heading towards the summit of Buchan Hill and look for a large outcrop called the **Grey Man of the Merrick**. It's a well-known landmark in these hills and resembles the face of a man.

② To your left is the ridge of Buchan Hill and to the right is White Brae and to the farside of that the Rig of the Jarkness. Do not cross the Gairland but keep going on the path to reach **Loch Valley**, skirting it to the west and then continue beside the **Mid Burn** to reach **Loch Neldricken**.

③ Head for the far west corner of the loch to find the infamous **Murder Hole** featured by S R Crockett in his novel *The Raiders* (1894). The story is based on a local legend that unwary travellers were robbed on these hills and their bodies disposed of in the loch.

④ From the Murder Hole head north, crossing a burn and then a wall. Pass to the east of the **Ewe Rig** and tiny **Loch Arron** and eventually reach the south side of **Loch Enoch**. Don't worry if the track vanishes or becomes indistinct, just keep heading north and you'll eventually reach the loch.

⑤ As you approach Loch Enoch you will see the outline of Mullwarchar beyond it and to the right. When you reach the loch go left and cross another wall. The slope in front of you is the **Redstone Rig** and although you have 1,000ft (305m) to climb it is not particularly taxing.

WHERE TO EAT AND DRINK ⓘ
Well this is the Galloway Hills and a pretty remote area. Not only is a picnic a good idea but by the time you've conquered Merrick you will feel in need of sustenance. The other options include a visit to the **Stroan Bridge tea room** (► Walk 10) and **The House O' Hill** at Bargrennan (► Walk 13).

⑥ From the summit cairn of **Merrick** head downhill towards a narrow ridge called the **Neive of the Spit** to reach the summit of **Benyellary**, the Hill of the Eagle. From here follow the footpath downhill beside a dry-stone wall then turn left and keep going downhill, into the forest, to reach the bothy at **Culsharg**. From there continue downhill to return to the car park.

WHILE YOU'RE THERE ⓘ
Take a trip to **Whithorn** where Christianity first arrived in Scotland towards the end of the 4th century. This is where St Ninian founded his early church Candida Casa, the White House, from where the name Whithorn comes. Once a popular place of pilgrimage, and a thriving community until pilgrimages were banned under pain of death after the Reformation, it is once again receiving attention because of recent archaeological discoveries. You can visit the interpretation centre, the dig and the old priory.

On the Trail of the Wigtown Martyrs

Visit the memorial to two women drowned at the stake for their religion.

•DISTANCE•	4 miles (6.4km)
•MINIMUM TIME•	3hrs
•ASCENT / GRADIENT•	98ft (30m)
•LEVEL OF DIFFICULTY•	
•PATHS•	Roads, old railway tracks and pavements
•LANDSCAPE•	River estuary, pasture and woodland
•SUGGESTED MAP•	aqua3 OS Explorer 311 Wigtown, Whithorn & The Machars
•START / FINISH•	Grid reference: NX 439547
•DOG FRIENDLINESS•	Keep on lead near livestock
•PARKING•	At Wigtown harbour
•PUBLIC TOILETS•	None on walk

BACKGROUND TO THE WALK

On 11 May 1685 two Wigtown women were dragged out on to the salt marshes near the town and tied to stakes. Eighteen-year-old Margaret Wilson and her companion, Margaret McLaughlan, aged 63, had been sentenced to death for their religious beliefs.

The Killing Times

This was during that period in Scots history known as the Killing Times when the Covenanters were persecuted for their beliefs. They were called Covenanters after a petition signed in Greyfriars churchyard in Edinburgh, in 1638, and thereafter in churches throughout the country. The covenant reaffirmed the belief of Scottish Presbyterians that there was a special relationship between God, as head of the Church, and the people. This ran contrary to the belief of the Stuart monarchy in the divine right of kings. Charles II sought to control the Church by appointing Episcopalian bishops and ministers. Presbyterian ministers were ousted from their churches, but simply took to the hills with their congregations and held open-air services called conventicles. Troops patrolled the hills and moors and if they came across these illegal meetings, broke them up by taking some worshippers prisoner and killing others on the spot.

Sentenced to Death

Margaret Wilson and Margaret McLaughlan were two Wigtownshire Covenanters who were tried in the tollbooth at Wigtown for rebellion and having taken part in several battles against the Crown. Found guilty they were sentenced to death by drowning and taken to the tidal Bladnoch River.

When they reached the execution site, the soldiers placed the older woman's stake further out in the estuary so that she would die first and thus terrify her younger companion to the point where she would yield and swear an oath to the King. But this was to no avail. While Margaret McLaughlan drowned the younger woman sung the 25th Psalm and then, as the water started to rise around her, began to pray out loud.

The water covered her as she prayed but after a while the soldiers pulled her up, revived her and asked her if she would pray for the King. A friend cried out to her urging her to say 'God save the King', but the only reply Margaret uttered was 'God save him if he will, for it is his salvation I desire.' On hearing this some of her relatives urged the commanding officer to release her. But he, drawing close to her, asked her to swear the oath or be returned to the water. She refused saying 'I will not, I am one of Christ's children, let me go'. But they would not let her go and she was again thrust under the water and held there until she died.

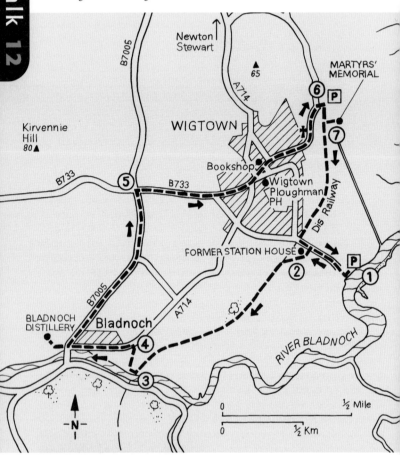

Walk 12 **Directions**

① Leave the car park, turn right and head uphill on a narrow country lane called **Harbour Road**. The house on the left near the top of the road was the former **station house** for Wigtown. Just before it there's a farm gate on the left. Go through it and on to a farm track.

② Follow the track to the point where it goes through another gate then veer right and climb up the old railway embankment. This has a good grassy surface along its entire length. Proceed along the embankment and through one gate.

③ A wall across the track will stop you at the point where the former railway bridge carried the track across the **River Bladnoch**. Turn right and go down the side of the embankment and cross a fence into a field. Veer right and head across the field to the far corner then go through a gate on to the main road.

WHERE TO EAT AND DRINK

The **Wigtown Ploughman** is one of the finest eating establishments in the region, with food that is out of this world. After a long walk refuel on a massive portion of mouthwatering Irish stew or the Wigtown Bay chowder made from freshly caught local fish. Fresh, high-quality local ingredients, a top chef and friendly staff are the key elements in the success of this family-run establishment. Children are welcome in the dining room.

---

④ Turn left and walk through the hamlet of **Bladnoch**. At the junction by a roundabout, cross the road to enter the **Bladnoch Distillery** car park. After visiting the distillery head back out of the car park and turn left at the roundabout. Continue along this road (the **B7005**) for approximately 1 mile (1.6km) until you get to a crossroads.

⑤ Turn right on to the **B733** and walk along it to reach **Wigtown**. When you reach the centre of the town bear left round the square and head towards the large and impressive former county buildings.

Pass them on your right, then the church and war memorial on your left and continue downhill. Eventually turn right into the car park for the Martyrs' Memorial.

⑥ Walk through the car park then turn left and make your way to the bird hide at the end of the path. From there retrace your steps to the car park and continue on the path leading to the **Martyrs' Memorial**. Turn left and walk out over the sands on a specially constructed wooden causeway to reach the memorial erected on the spot where the two women were drowned.

⑦ Return to the path and turn left. Go through a kissing gate then another gate, which is slightly below the level you are walking on and to the left. At the end of the path go through another gate in front of the old **station house** turn left on to **Harbour Road** and return to the car park.

WHILE YOU'RE THERE

Don't miss a visit to the **Bookshop** in North Mains Street. It has the largest stock of secondhand books in Scotland, displayed in a Georgian building that is a labyrinth of rooms crammed with floor-to-ceiling bookshelves. Comfortable seats can be found in odd corners and by the fire where browsers can sit and, well, browse. The coffee is always on and always fresh. And it's free.

WHAT TO LOOK FOR

The salt marshes along the last section of the walk are rich in plant and animal life. Look for **eel grass**, the only flowering plant that can grow under the sea, and **glasswort** which used to be burned and its ashes used in glass production. You may spot **curlews** wading in the marshes using their long curved beaks to probe the mud for the tiny invertebrates that inhabit the creeks and pools.

The Wells of the Rees

Take this strenuous walk along the Southern Upland Way in search of the past.

Walk 13

•DISTANCE•	6¼ miles (10.1km)
•MINIMUM TIME•	3hrs 30min
•ASCENT / GRADIENT•	558ft (170m) ▲▲▲
•LEVEL OF DIFFICULTY•	🚶 🚶 🚶
•PATHS•	Forest roads, forest track, very rough ground
•LANDSCAPE•	Hills, forest and loch
•SUGGESTED MAP•	aqua3 OS Explorer 310 Glenluce & Kirkcowan
•START / FINISH•	Grid reference: NX 260735
•DOG FRIENDLINESS•	OK but keep on lead near livestock
•PARKING•	Near Derry farm
•PUBLIC TOILETS•	None on route

BACKGROUND TO THE WALK

Sitting 'on the hillside at the back of the sheiling called Kilgallioch' wrote Davie Bell, 'are three dome-shaped structures of great antiquity.' These were the Wells o' the Rees, the rees in question being sheep pens surrounding the wells.

A Determined Effort

Davie Bell, popularly known as The Highwayman, rode his bicycle all over the roughest parts of south west Scotland in the 1930s and 40s and chronicled his exploits in a weekly column in the *Ayrshire Post* (► Walk 11). He was intrigued by the Wells o' the Rees and mounted several expeditions in search of them. Although he came close, time and again he was defeated by thick bracken and an almost featureless landscape. Today, the waymarked Southern Upland Way (SUW) takes walkers to within 100yds (91m) of the wells and a signpost points them out. But when Davie Bell was roaming these moors, often on his bicycle, but sometimes on foot, there were no long distance footpaths or signposts. Many paths and tracks would have criss-crossed the moor but they were the tracks used by herdsmen and farmers to their remote steadings.

Davie eventually found the wells after getting directions from the farmer's wife at Killgallioch (► Walk 14). He described them as 'three piles of stones… skilfully constructed, with each well having a canopy and the shape of the whole like that of a beehive.' Made of flat stones and oval in shape they were 'streamlined into the hillside, with a recess over the well for a utensil.' Sixty years later the people are gone but the wells remain.

This part of Galloway was sparsely populated before the forestry came, but when trees replaced sheep, shepherds and their families abandoned their lonely sheilings to ruin and decay amidst the trees. With the opening of the SUW, walkers trudge this wild landscape once again. These latter day pilgrims, follow in the footsteps of early Christians on their way to Whithorn. Although locals told Davie Bell that the wells had been built by the Romans, it seems more likely that they were made for the pilgrims. According to the Revd C H Dick in his *Highways and Byways of Galloway and Carrick*, the wells may have been part of the ancient church and graveyard of Killgallioch, which was sited near by, although he walked across the moors from New Luce in 1916 and saw nothing in the way of ruins. The pilgrims' route to Whithorn was also the path followed by lepers on their way from Glenluce Abbey to the leper colony 1½ miles (2.4km) north of Loch Derry at Libberland. They washed in the Purgatory Burn near Laggangarn and no doubt stopped for refreshment at the Wells o' the Rees.

Walk 13 Directions

① Cross a cattle grid and head west along the SUW on a well-surfaced forest road. Pass **Loch Derry**, on your right in just under a mile

(1.6km), then continue on the forest road, passing a signpost on the left to **Linn's Tomb**.

② Follow the road as it curves to the right and then, following the SUW markerpost, turn left, leave the road and head uphill. It's a rather steep climb from here, on a fairly well-trodden path with plenty of waymarkers.

③ Cross a forest road and continue on the uphill path heading towards the summit of **Craig Airie Fell**. Reach the summit at an Ordnance Survey trig point.

WHAT TO LOOK FOR ℹ
Coming off Craigmoddie Fell look for the box-like stone enclosure containing the **tomb** of Alexander Linn. He was a Covenanter during the dark years of the 'Killing Times' (▶ Walk 12). Discovered near the summit of the fell in 1685, by a party of soldiers led by Lieutenant General Drummond, Linn was executed without trial. You'll have to use the stones jutting out of the wall to gain access to the enclosure.

④ From the OS **triangulation pillar**, continue on a well-marked path towards a waymarker on the horizon. Turn left at the waymarker and head downhill on a footpath that twists and turns to another waymarker near the bottom. Turn right here on to another obvious trail and keep going to reach the edge of the forest.

⑤ The SUW now follows a forest ride. A short distance along here you will come to a clearing with a cairn on your left-hand side. Keep

WHILE YOU'RE THERE ℹ
Visit the 12th-century **Cistercian abbey** at Glenluce. This was founded in 1190 by the Earl of Galloway and was an important stopping point for pilgrims on the way to Whithorn. Only the chapter house still has its vaulted medieval roof, the rest is a ruin which, over the years, has been used as a source of local building materials.

straight ahead following the direction arrows on the waymarkers to the next clearing where a sign points left to the **Wells of the Rees**. Turn left and head downhill, through bracken, across a ruined dry-stone wall, through more bracken and then a gap in another wall. In wintertime you will find the wells easily but in summer, when the bracken is thick, you'll have to poke about a bit. The first two wells are on your right as you come through the gap and the other is off to the left.

⑥ Retrace your steps from here to the signpost and turn right. Retrace your steps to the edge of the forest and turn right, following the edge of the forest and a burn, slightly downhill to a fence. Cross this and head roughly west across rough and boggy ground towards **Craigmoddie Fell**.

WHERE TO EAT AND DRINK ℹ
This is very remote country and as this is a strenuous walk it is advisable to carry food and drink with you to eat along the way. The nearest eating establishment is **The House O' Hill Hotel** at Bargrennan, which welcomes children. It is a considerable distance from the start and you'll find several alternatives at **Newton Stewart**.

⑦ Climb to the highest point then look to your left to Loch Derry then, to the right of it, Derry farm. Head in a straight line for **Derry farm** then drop down off the fell and pick up a path heading towards **Loch Derry**.

⑧ Follow this to a small patch of trees, through a gate and on to the forest road. Turn right and return to **Derry farm** and the start of the walk.

The Standing Stones of Laggangarn

Prehistoric relic on the Pilgrims route to Whithorn.
See map and information panel for Walk 13

•DISTANCE•	2½ miles (4km)
•MINIMUM TIME•	1hr 30min
•ASCENT / GRADIENT•	115ft (35m) ▲▲▲
•LEVEL OF DIFFICULTY•	🚶🚶 🚶🚶 🚶🚶

Walk 14 Directions (Walk 13 option)

From the signpost (Point Ⓐ) go straight ahead on the SUW towards **Laggangarn**. Follow this to the wooden bridge over the **Tarf Water** then head uphill to the **Standing Stones of Laggangarn**. Originally part of a stone circle they have stood here for about 5,000 years and were on the main pilgrims' route from Edinburgh to Whithorn. Those early Christians incised crosses on the stones, adopting them for their own purposes. As you stand before them consider that over the centuries countless thousands have stood on this same spot, among them Robert the Bruce and Mary, Queen of Scots.

After the stones the track drops down to a clearing at the ruins of Laggangarn and the odd looking **Beehive bothy**. On this remote patch of moor this offers the only shelter and is a convenient spot for lunch. While you eat, read the entries in the visitors' book and decide whether to continue or retrace your steps back to the **Wells of the Rees**.

With the front door of the Beehive to your back, go ahead then veer left towards a gap in the trees. The going gets tough from here as you encounter rough, uneven and often boggy ground. Cross a wire fence, then a burn and turn left to follow the line of a ruined wall and the course of the burn. Follow this, ignoring a forest ride to the right, to come to a bend in the burn. Turn right on to the forest ride and head along it, round a dog-leg to the left and then turn left at a T-junction. Cross the remains of an old wall then, just before a clearing, look to the left to see if you can spot the remains of the farm of **Killgallioch**. The Highwayman, Davie Bell, arrived here in the 1940s having cycled over the moors. He was seeking directions for the Wells of the Rees (► Walk 13), which were not then conveniently signposted.

Cross the clearing, go through a gap in the wall then turn left and head uphill. Cross another wall and go uphill through a forest ride. At the point where it appears blocked by thick bushes carefully enter the forest to the right and circle round. When the ride intersects the SUW turn right and continue to the your outward route at Point Ⓑ.

Castle Kennedy Gardens

Discover the gardens around the ancient stronghold of a powerful family.

•DISTANCE•	6 miles (9.7km)
•MINIMUM TIME•	3hrs 30min
•ASCENT / GRADIENT•	49ft (15m) ▲ ▲ ▲
•LEVEL OF DIFFICULTY•	🚶 🚶 🚶
•PATHS•	Estate roads, lanes, minor road and rough paths, 1 stile
•LANDSCAPE•	Estate woodlands, lochside and pastures
•SUGGESTED MAP•	aqua3 OS Explorer 309 Stranraer & The Rhins
•START / FINISH•	Grid reference: NX 108597
•DOG FRIENDLINESS•	Dogs should be kept on leads
•PARKING•	On-street parking in Castle Kennedy, opposite gardens
•PUBLIC TOILETS•	None on route

Walk 15 Directions

This is the ancient parish of Inch, a burgh of Barony since the 17th-century and once a major stronghold of the Kennedy family, from which the ruined castle and the village take their names. The Kennedys of that period were a much feared and powerful family.

Walk towards the **A75 Euro Route**, cross it and go through the main entrance to **Castle Kennedy Gardens**. This is part of the Southern Upland Way (SUW) and follows the main drive into the gardens. Go over a crossroads and follow the drive as it turns left and heads along the banks of the **White Loch** (or Loch of Inch). On the east bank is Lochinch Castle built in the Scottish baronial style in 1867 and the current home of the Earl and Countess of Stair. Continue along the road, following the waymarks, as the road passes the entrance to Castle Kennedy Gardens, for which there is an admission charge.

Castle Kennedy Gardens were created on 75 acres (30ha) of land around the ruins of Castle Kennedy, which was burnt down in 1716. They were the creation of the 2nd Earl of Stair who, as British Ambassador to France, had been inspired by the gardens at Versailles. The earl had been one of Marlborough's generals in the War of the Spanish Succession (1701–14) and this enabled him to acquire the use of troops from the Inniskilling Fusiliers and Royal Scots Greys to transform the peninsula between the White and Black lochs into the gardens you can see today.

From the entrance bridge to the gardens turn right and head uphill to reach a T-junction. Turn left on to a country lane then take the next left beside a lodge. Follow this estate road through woodland along the banks of the **Black Loch** (or Loch Crindil). To your left is a small wooded island shown on the maps as Heron Isle. This is a crannog, an artificial island created in prehistoric times as a habitation,

> ### WHERE TO EAT AND DRINK ⓘ
> The **Plantings Inn** at Castle Kennedy village is a modern pub with a relaxing and pleasant atmosphere. It's a favoured pit stop for many of the countless hundreds of walkers who pass here each year on the Southern Upland Way. The friendly staff serve food all day and the beer on tap is Bellhaven, one of Scotland's finest real ales.

which would afford protection from wild animals and marauding tribes. Look out on this stretch for some of the many birds that can be seen near the water's edge. The lochs are a haven for species such as grebes, ducks and geese.

At a junction near the head of the loch turn left and cross a bridge. You will shortly reach a crossroads. Go straight ahead and, at the next crossroads, go right and follow this road until it reaches a T-junction beside another estate lodge.

> ### WHILE YOU'RE THERE ⓘ
> The **Tropic House**, at Carty Port between Newton Stewart and Wigtown is a must for anyone interested in, or curious about, carnivorous plants. This is the finest collection on display anywhere in the United Kingdom. Visitors can also walk through a tropical setting and watch free flying exotic butterflies.

When the earl was creating his garden he first built a huge, round pond then installed some terraces and embankments and had them planted with a bewildering variety of botanical specimens. There are avenues flanked by trees grown from seeds, dazzling displays of azaleas, rhododendrons and spectacular embothriums, more commonly known as Chilean fire bushes. A country trail with numbered posts runs through the garden guiding visitors to some of the best parts including the avenue of monkey puzzle trees, which is at least 100 years old.

Leave the estate and turn left on to a country lane and look out for a track on the left about ½ mile (800m) along. Turn left, continue along this farm track until it terminates at a T-junction on another estate road and turn right. To your left is a graveyard and the remains of the old church of Inch, which is worthy of a closer look. Behind it is the **White Loch**, or Loch of Inch, and the small island of Inch Crindil.

The estate road ends at a T-junction beside another lodge. Cross the **A75 Euro Route**. On the other side pass the modern Inch church and continue along a minor road which runs beside it.

Look out on the right for a stile about 100yds (91m) before a railway bridge. Turn left over the stile and rejoin the SUW. Running parallel to the line of the Stranraer-to-Girvan railway, this well-defined footpath through the woods eventually reaches a SUW interpretation board by a house near the edge of the village. Continue to the end of the path at its junction with the road and go straight ahead. Turn left at the next junction and return to your car.

> ### WHAT TO LOOK FOR ⓘ
> Try and catch a glimpse of the ruins of the old **castle**, which are visible from several points on the walk. This early 17th-century pile was considerably extended throughout its life and had a five-storey central block with flanking turrets and towers plus two double storey 18th-century additions.

Port Logan or Fictional Ronansay?

A picturesque fishing village where everything is not as it seems.

•DISTANCE•	3 miles (4.8km)
•MINIMUM TIME•	2hrs
•ASCENT / GRADIENT•	492ft (150m) ▲ ▲ ▲
•LEVEL OF DIFFICULTY•	林 林 林
•PATHS•	Shoreline, country lanes and hill tracks, 1 stile
•LANDSCAPE•	Hill, pasture and shoreline
•SUGGESTED MAP•	aqua3 OS Explorer 309 Stranraer & The Rhins
•START / FINISH•	Grid reference: NX 097411
•DOG FRIENDLINESS•	No problems but keep on lead near livestock
•PARKING•	Public car park on road to Logan Fish Pond
•PUBLIC TOILETS•	At car park

BACKGROUND TO THE WALK

The couple standing by a building beside the harbour at Port Logan were perplexed. Pointing to a ferry timetable on a notice board on the wall they asked a passing villager, 'Can you really get a ferry from here to Skye?' The local just smiled and pointed to the sign on the building, which declared it to be Ronansay Primary School. 'It's just a set for the television people,' he told them.

Film Location

Like other visitors to this picturesque village, the couple could be excused for feeling a wee bit confused. Walk along the main street and go down some steps to the McPhee Stores. It looks like a thriving village shop. Lining the wall along the front are racks of fresh vegetables, crates of lemonade bottles, plastic buckets and spades and the fishing nets beloved of small children on holiday at the seaside. But open the door to this village store and post office and you'd get a surprise. For the racks of birthday cards and shelves of merchandise visible from the outside barely conceal a garage door. The shop is just a façade. Small clues give the game away like the advert for the *Oban Times* beside the door and window stickers advertising the *West Highland Free Press*. For Port Logan is the television double for the fictional island of Ronansay in the series *Two Thousand Acres of Sky*.

Fictional Ronansay

In the BBC television series Ronansay is just off the coast of Skye and its islanders are trying to attract new blood into their community. To save the village school from closure, they need two new children. Michelle Collins stars as a young mother, desperate to escape from a seedy, inner city housing estate, who sees the Ronansay advert and decides it's just what she needs. The only problem is that the islanders are looking for a family and Abby, Michelle's character, is a single mother. She needs to find a husband. She talks her best pal, Kenny, played by Paul Kaye, the comedian, into pretending to be her husband and going to live in Ronansay with her and the kids.

Glorious Scenery

In the outdoor scenes, shot in and around Port Logan, the glorious Galloway scenery takes over as the main star. Nearby Portpatrick masquerades as Skye and other locations include Dunskey Castle, Drummore and Stranraer.

Not surprisingly, given the popularity of the series, many extra visitors are attracted to Port Logan and are thrilled if they arrive while the production company is shooting. Other visitors who are not aware of the village's double life just try to figure out if the local hotel is called the Raeburn or the Port Logan Inn. Sometimes it can be both in the course of a week.

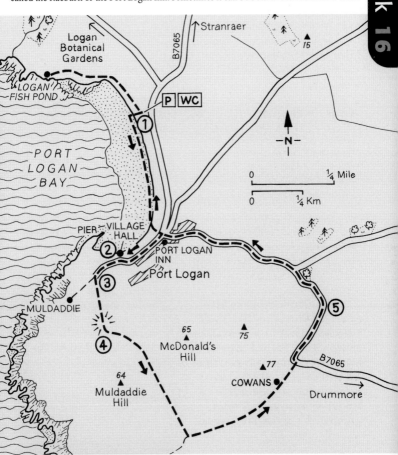

Walk 16 Directions

① From the car park go across a wooden walkway, down some steps on to the beach and turn left to walk along the beach. When you reach the start of the village climb on to the road in front of the **Port Logan Inn**. Turn right and continue along the main street, passing the war memorial to reach the **village hall**. In *Two Thousand Acres of Sky* the village hall features as the village school, and has a school sign fixed to the front. There's also a timetable for Caledonian MacBrayne ferries displayed on a notice board on the wall. Opposite the village hall is a small but picturesque harbour with a rather unusual lighthouse. Nowadays, when it is not in use as a film location, Port Logan harbour is used only by a few pleasure craft.

② This was a thriving fishing port in the past and the pier once again looks as though it is busy, festooned with fishing gear, gas bottles and sacks of coal. Although they are all real, they are only there as props. Move away from the harbour area and along the road to the farm of **Muldaddie**.

WHILE YOU'RE THERE ⓘ

Do not miss a visit to **Logan Botanical Gardens**. Benefiting from the Gulf Stream this is described as 'Scotland's most exotic garden' because of the varied collections of weird and unusual plants. Huge clumps of giant gunnera, groves of eucalypts and enormous Scots thistles jostle for position with more common specimens. In the discovery centre are displays covering the history of this fascinating area.

---

③ Just before the farm turn left on to an old hill track and head uphill. Near the top look back downhill for a magnificent view back to the village and across Port Logan Bay to the Mull of Logan. The track is heavily overgrown here, and is blocked by a barrier made from gates, but this can easily be crossed by a stile at the side.

④ Continue along the track to a T-junction. Turn left, go through a gate and head along a farm road to

---

WHERE TO EAT AND DRINK ⓘ

One of the best eating establishments in the area is the **Mariners** pub at nearby Drummore. It's a friendly place with a quaint old world atmosphere and the food is superb. It serves a variety of meals and snacks including a huge and hearty breakfast. Not to be missed are the superb seafood dishes made from fresh local produce at a fraction of what it would cost you elsewhere.

Cowans farm. Continue through the farm steading and reach the end of the road at a T-junction. Turn left on to the **B7065** and head downhill.

⑤ Follow this winding road back to **Port Logan** then go back on to the beach, turn right and retrace your steps to the car park. From here you can continue along a rough road to the **Logan Fish Pond**. It's right at the end on the left and is by the only building there.

WHAT TO LOOK FOR ⓘ

A little white Victorian bathing hut stands beside the **Logan Fish Pond**, once a favourite spot for an outing by the folks in the big house. There's an admission charge to get in but it is worth it to try hand feeding the fish. Two centuries ago this was a live fish larder created using a natural formation on the shore.

Ardstinchar Castle

The Ayrshire Tragedy, a murder most foul.

•DISTANCE•	3 miles (4.8km)
•MINIMUM TIME•	2hrs
•ASCENT / GRADIENT•	295ft (90m) ▲▲ ▲ ▲
•LEVEL OF DIFFICULTY•	🚶🚶 🚶🚶 🚶🚶
•PATHS•	Country lanes and farm tracks
•LANDSCAPE•	Hillside, pastures and seashore
•SUGGESTED MAP•	aqua3 OS Explorer 317 Ballantrae, Barr & Barrhill
•START / FINISH•	Grid reference: NX 082824
•DOG FRIENDLINESS•	Mainly farmland so keep on lead near livestock
•PARKING•	Car park near school on Foreland, Ballantrae
•PUBLIC TOILETS•	Beside car park

BACKGROUND TO THE WALK

Ballantrae once had quite a reputation as a place where strange and gruesome events took place. If the ruins of Ardstinchar Castle could speak they would tell a tale of greed and avarice, of cousins involved in a deadly feud and a series of events designed to wipe out one branch of Ayrshire's most powerful family, the Kennedys.

Fact or Fiction?

An ancient manuscript lies in a dusty basement in an Edinburgh library. It was written at the time of these events and, although the author remains anonymous, it is believed to be the work of John Mure of Auchindrain House near Ayr. It was the writing of S R Crocket, minister turned novelist, who brought this story to the attention of a wider public when he took it and used it as the basis of his novel *The Grey Man*. This is a work of fiction but woven through the tale is the factual thread of the tragic events which occurred in Ayrshire during the turbulent years at the end of the 16th century.

Kennedy Feud

Although Crocket's novel opens with a fiction, the burning of Ardstincher Castle, he uses this event to outline the origins of the Kennedy feud. This was an attempt by the Earl of Cassillis, the senior Kennedy, to acquire the lands of Crossraguel Abbey. All efforts to persuade Allan Stewart, the Commendator of Crossraguel having failed, Cassillis seized him, carried him off to his stronghold at Dunure Castle and there in the Black Vault of Dunure 'roasted the hapless Stewart over a slow fire until he signed.' However, Stewart's brother in law, Kennedy of Bargany, rescued him and although Cassillis was brought before the High Court and made to compensate Stewart he was allowed to keep the lands he had obtained. Cassillis was thereafter intent on destroying the house of Bargany and various plots, intrigues and blood lettings took place culminating in the murder of Bargany by Cassillis near Maybole in 1601.

Bargany was interred in the family vault at Ballantrae and, although Cassillis escaped justice again, Bargany's ally John Mure, the Grey Man of Crocket's tale, took revenge by having an uncle of Cassillis assassinated. Suspicion immediately fell on Mure but he had an alibi. However, there was one witness who could tie Mure to the crime. A young boy had delivered a letter from the intended victim to Mure who read it then told the boy to return it and say he had not found Mure. To protect himself, Mure and his son strangled the hapless boy and threw him into the sea near Girvan. The boys' body washed ashore just a few days later, both Mures were arrested, tried and found guilty of that murder and also of being involved in the assassination. Sentenced to death for their crimes, father and son were both executed at Edinburgh in 1611, thus ending the feud and leaving Cassillis once more free of any retribution.

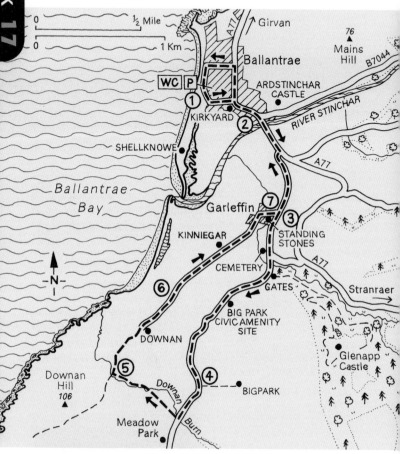

Walk 17 Directions

① Leave the car park and turn left on to the **Foreland**. At the T-junction with **Main Street** cross the road and turn right. Near the outskirts of the village, just before the bridge over the **River Stinchar**, look up to your left to view the

ruins of the former stronghold of the Bargany Kennedy's **Ardstinchar Castle**. As the walls are considered unstable it is perhaps not advisable to go any closer.

② From here cross the **Stinchar Bridge** and take the first turning on the right, heading uphill on a narrow country lane and past a row

Walk 17

of cottages. At a junction in the road keep to the left but look out for one of the **Garleffin Standing Stones** in the rear garden of the bungalow at the junction.

③ There's another stone in the front garden of this house but you will see that later in the walk. In the meantime continue uphill passing the cemetery, on your right, **Glenapp Castle** gates on your left and a little further on the **Big Park Civic Amenity Site**, on the left.

④ The next landmark on the left is the farm road to **Bigpark**. Continue past this and look out for the next farmhouse on the right. About 300yds (274m) before this house the road dips; there's a stream beside the road here. Turn right on to a farm track that heads downhill between two high hedges.

⑤ Near the bottom of the hill, just past a large barn on your left, the road splits. Turn right here and

continue along this road, through a farm steading, past **Downan farmhouse** and uphill. When the road levels out look to the horizon in front of you for the distinctive outline of Knockdolian Hill, often referred to by local mariners as the 'false Craig'.

⑥ Look over to your left at the same time to see the real Ailsa Craig away to the north west. Looking along the beach towards Ballantrae is Shellknowe. Continue along this road, past the farm of **Kinniegar** and through the hamlet of **Garleffin**. Note that some of the houses have names like Druidslea and Glendruid.

⑦ In the front garden of **Druidslea** is another standing stone. Turn left, go downhill on this country lane, turn left on to the main road and return to **Ballantrae**. Go through a gate on the left-hand side and into the kirkyard. The Kennedy crypt can be found by going up some steps on the right. If the door is locked you can still see inside through a small window on the door. Return to **Main Street** and turn right, go along the street and take the first turning left past the library. Walk along this street to reach the T-junction and turn left into **Foreland** and return to the car park where you started.

Byne Hill and the Firth of Clyde

Enjoy the views across the sea to Ailsa Craig, the source of the world's curling stones.

•DISTANCE•	3¾ miles (6km)
•MINIMUM TIME•	3hrs
•ASCENT / GRADIENT•	571ft (174m) ▲▲▲
•LEVEL OF DIFFICULTY•	🚶 🚶 🚶
•PATHS•	Farm roads, dirt tracks and open hillside, 1 stile
•LANDSCAPE•	Hill, pasture, woodland and seaside
•SUGGESTED MAP•	aqua3 OS Explorer 317 Ballantrae, Barr & Barrhill
•START / FINISH•	Grid reference: NX 187955
•DOG FRIENDLINESS•	Keep on lead, this is sheep country
•PARKING•	On road beside Girvan cemetery
•PUBLIC TOILETS•	None on route

BACKGROUND TO THE WALK

The lone sentinel of Ailsa Craig in the Firth of Clyde, which dominates the seaward views on this walk, is the plug of a volcano, extinct since prehistoric times. First mentioned in the charters of the Abbey of Crossraguel in 1404 as the Insula de Ailsay, the island was part of that estate until the Reformation in 1560. Since then it has belonged to the Cassillis family, and has given its name to the senior family member, the Marquis of Ailsa. To generations of immigrant Irish it was known simply as Paddy's Milestone as it is located approximately half way between Belfast and Glasgow. But Ailsa Craig's main claim to fame is as the source of granite used in the world's supply of curling stones.

The Finest Granite

The fine micro-granite from Ailsa Craig has been used to make curling stones since the beginning of the 19th century. On the island there are several kinds of granite, Common Ailsa, Blue Hone and Red Hone. All three have been used in curling stone manufacture but the Blue Hone, a finer grained variety, produced the best running surface. Quarrying stopped in 1971 and Welsh granite was substituted in the manufacturing process. But each stone still had what was known as an Ailsert, a small coaster of Ailsa Craig Blue Hone granite, inserted in the base.

A Family Business

Originally, quarrying on the island was carried out by the Girvan family, who had a lease from the Marquis of Ailsa. They lived in a cottage on the island during the summer months, blasting and extracting the rock for transport back to Girvan harbour and onwards to the curling stone factory in Mauchline. A small railway line was built to carry the rocks to the island pier for loading on to small fishing boats.

During the summer Ailsa Craig was a busy place. As well as the resident lighthouse keepers, the Girvan family and their workforce, there was a constant stream of day trippers on cruises from Girvan harbour. They could climb to the small ruined castle, take a tour of the lighthouse and wander around the island. Mrs Girvan supplied afternoon teas in a small café. By the 1950s the Girvans had given up quarrying, shut the café and removed their sheep and goats, leaving the rock to the lighthouse keepers and the birds.

Kays of Mauchline, the world's only manufacturer of curling stones, started using Welsh Trevor granite to produce their stones with the Ailsert to preserve the smooth running surface. However, in the summer of 2002, Kays removed some 1,500 tons of granite boulders from the old quarries on the island. No blasting or quarrying took place. They simply collected what was already there to avoid disturbing the island's population of seabirds. Now they will once more make curling stones entirely from Ailsa Craig granite.

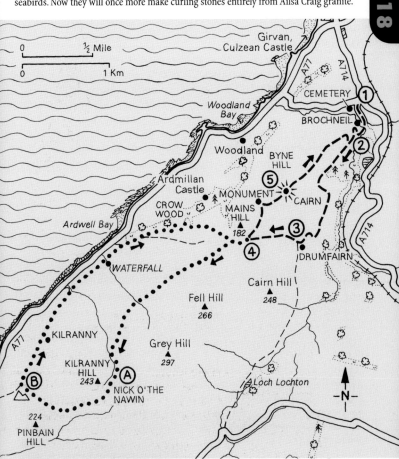

Walk 18 Directions

① Go along the road to **Brochneil farm** which runs along the east side of the cemetery. Continue on this through Brochneil steading, then cross a wooden bridge. Go through a gate, over a stone bridge and follow the road uphill, as it turns first right, then left.

② This is the farm road to **Drumfairn**, formerly the shepherd's house for Woodland farm, now part of the Scottish Wildlife Trust Grey

Hill Grasslands Wildlife Reserve. Cross a cattle grid, go through two gates then, at a third cattle grid, cross a stile and go left towards Drumfairn steading.

③ The house at Drumfairn has been damaged by fire and is derelict. Do not enter it as it is in a dangerous condition. Turn right at the steading and, keeping the sheep pens on your left, walk ahead. Go through a gate then cross a wire fence near another gate. Go through this gate and head right, across the field. When you reach the fence turn left and follow it to its junction with a tumbledown wall. Cross here and, keeping the fence on your right, head along the edge of the field. Cross a small burn near some sheep rees (pens) and continue following the line of the fence until you come to a gate.

WHERE TO EAT AND DRINK ⓘ

The **Ailsa Arms Hotel** in nearby Girvan serves a full range of snacks and bar meals and has an excellent restaurant menu. Their fish and chips are particularly tasty after a long day out on the hills. The friendly staff of this family-run establishment ensure that everyone gets a warm welcome.

---

④ Go through the gate then go right, cross a small burn and continue along a faint track heading for the saddle between **Mains Hill** on your left-hand side and **Byne Hill** on your right. Take time to visit the **monument** which was erected to the memory of Archibald C B Craufurd of Ardmillan Estate. As the monument is in poor repair keep a safe distance from it. There used to be a plaque on the front, but some years ago this was removed and dumped in the woods below. Retrace your steps a short

---

WHILE YOU'RE THERE ⓘ

Visit **Culzean Castle and Country Park** a few miles north along the coast road. This Adam masterpiece was built for the Marquis of Ailsa, senior member of the Kennedy family, who gifted it to the nation just after World War Two. American President, Dwight D Eisenhower was given use of rooms within the castle for life and these rooms are now on view to the public. A display traces his links with the house. Various events are held in the country park.

---

distance and turn left through a gap in the wall and head up the side of **Byne Hill** to reach a prominent commemorative cairn at the summit. From this vantage point there is one of the finest views of the Firth of Clyde. On a clear day you can see the Antrim coast of Northern Ireland, the island of Arran and the Mull of Kintyre to the north and west, and, about 8 miles (12.9km) out in the sea, the distinctive outline of Ailsa Craig, the plug of an extinct volcano and the source of granite for curling stones.

⑤ With the cairn at your back, walk straight ahead. Cross a saddle between the summit and the lower part of the hill, keeping at first to the higher ground then descending towards the north east side of the hill where the footpath ends at a kissing gate. Go through this gate and turn left on to the farm road. Retrace your steps from here to return to the start.

WHAT TO LOOK FOR ⓘ

From the summit of the Byne Hill, looking north you will see some tall white buildings situated on the northern outskirts of Girvan. This is **Grant's Whisky Distillery** where their popular brand Standfast is distilled.

Kilranny Hill and Steading

An extension takes you over rough ground to a ruined and forsaken shepherd's dwelling.
See map and information panel for Walk 18

•DISTANCE•	4¼ miles (6.8km)
•MINIMUM TIME•	3hrs
•ASCENT / GRADIENT•	853ft (260m) ▲▲▲
•LEVEL OF DIFFICULTY•	눈눈 눈

Walk 19 Directions (Walk 18 option)

From the gate (Point ④ on Walk 18) continue along the fence towards a clump of gorse. Go round this and arrive at another gate. From here strike uphill at an angle of 45 degrees towards a gate in the fence. Go through the gate and continue along the flank of the hill. As you reach the high ground a solitary ash tree will be visible ahead to the left. Heading towards this, go through a gate and follow the line of an old wall.

Follow a faint track left from the wall near a burn, keeping the burn on your left and the ash tree ahead. Just beyond the tree, turn left through a gate and head up towards a gap between the hills called the **Nick o' the Nawin**, (Point Ⓐ). Go through the Nick and round **Kilranny Hill** until Pinbain Hill looms ahead. Make towards Pinbain, cross the dry-stone wall at a gate and turn right, following the wall downhill, through a gate then steeply down to the old coach road, (Point Ⓑ). In the 19th century, this was the main road to Stranraer. Turn right down the road.

Go through two gates and pass the ruin of **Kilranny**. As late as the 1960s, the families here used candles and oil lamps, while a coal fire was used for warmth and cooking. At sheep clipping time, the small enclosure beside the sheep pens would be ringed with wooden clipping benches each straddled by a shepherd. It was a lively scene, particularly when the farmer arrived with a crate of beer.

Leave the ruin with its ghosts of long gone herds and head downhill. At a hairpin bend go straight ahead along a farm track. Go through a gate near a waterfall then right on to a farm road heading uphill.

When the road forks, take the right fork uphill. At the next fork go left and follow this road, going through one gate, to its end. Now follow the edge of the woods on your left round a double horseshoe to the **Crow Wood**. Go through two gates here then head diagonally right across the field and uphill until you reach a wall. Follow this to the corner of the field and cross a burn to two gates at right angles. With the dry-stone wall on your left, go through the gate in front of you. Circle the gorse then retrace your steps to the gate at Point ④.

Walk 20

Up the Howe of Laggan

The story of a young shepherd's selfless sacrifice.

•DISTANCE•	8 miles (12.9km)
•MINIMUM TIME•	4hrs
•ASCENT / GRADIENT•	676ft (206m) ▲▲▲
•LEVEL OF DIFFICULTY•	👫 👫 👫
•PATHS•	Forest roads
•LANDSCAPE•	Hill and forest
•SUGGESTED MAP•	aqua3 OS Explorer 317 Ballantrae, Barr & Barrhill
•START / FINISH•	Grid reference: NX 287942
•DOG FRIENDLINESS•	Sheep everywhere, essential that dogs are kept on leads
•PARKING•	Barr Hill Walks car park
•PUBLIC TOILETS•	Barr village

Walk 20 Directions

From the car park head back downhill and turn left at the T-junction. Continue along the forest road to the entrance to **Changue House**. Where the road forks just past here, keep right. To the left, at the fork in the road, is an old, tumbledown building that used to be a shepherd's dwelling. This was where the McTaggart family lived just before World War One. The father and his sons were all noted shepherds in the area.

There was a blizzard raging early on the morning of 11 January 1913 when Christopher (Kirstie) McTaggart rose. He breakfasted then announced that he was off to the hills to check on his flock.

> **WHERE TO EAT AND DRINK** ⓘ
> Try the local **hotel** in the village of Barr, the **Ailsa Arms Hotel** in Girvan or, if you want something a bit more up-market, try **Wilding's Restaurant** in Girvan's Montgomery Street. It's just across the road from the Ailsa Arms.

Go through a gate and continue for 100yds (91m). At the fork in the road go left and downhill beside the **Water of Gregg** following the blue and yellow waymarkers. Go right through another gate and keep on the forest road. Cross a bridge and continue along the opposite side of **Gregg Water**.

This was the route that 19-year-old Kirstie trudged along on that morning. Head bowed into the storm he worked his way steadily uphill, his dog by his side. The landscape here was considerably different at the beginning of the 20th century. There were no conifer plantations to provide shelter or to break the force of a wild and bitter wind. The land for miles around was bare hillside broken only by a network of dry-stone walls.

When the path divides near a bridge go right and follow the red waymarkers and the sign pointing towards Kirstie's Trail. You are now approaching the Howe of Laggan a wild and lonely valley in Kirstie's day. Here he expected to find his

Walk 20

sheep, sheltering he hoped, in their pens. Those which may be buried in the snow would have to be dug out. It's not known if he had to rescue any sheep because Kirstie never returned from the Howe of Laggan. Concerned about his missing brother his twin, Davie, and a couple of friends went up Gregg Water in search of Kirstie.

> **WHILE YOU'RE THERE**   ⓘ
> Visit the ruined **church** at Old Dailly with its Covenanter stones. High on the gable of the church is a plaque dedicated to William Bell Scott, the Pre-Raphaelite painter and poet who lived at Penkill Castle and is buried in the churchyard.

They found him lying by the sheep pens, still alive but in the advanced stages of hypothermia. In vain they attempted to restore the heat to his frozen body but he died 15 minutes after they found him.

At the next junction turn right and then immediately right again on to a footpath. Cross a bridge and go through a small gate to enter the enclosure at **Kirstie's Cairn**. A picnic table makes this the ideal spot for a pit stop.

Because the weather was dreadful they were unable to bring Kirstie's body home so they left it where it had fallen, near the present cairn. The dog refused to leave his master and stood guard over the body. Next day the storm had abated and a party of 20 or so brought Kirstie back from the Howe of Laggan.

Return via the footbridge and path to the forest road. Turn left then right and follow the yellow waymarkers. The road climbs here for a fair distance with great views along the Howe of Laggan and once

on the top you should be able to see the pass of the Nick of the Balloch in the distance.

At Kirstie's funeral the minister, the Revd John Angus, suggested that the young men of the community raise a memorial to his memory. Kirstie's Cairn was erected a few paces from the spot where he died.

When the road forks keep left and uphill. Follow green cycle route waymarks which are frequent on this section. At the next junction keep right and continue uphill. Eventually reach the top of the hill and continue on the road down the other side. Yellow waymarkers will reappear although there is a fair distance with no waymarkers. However it is virtually impossible to get lost on this walk. Eventually reach another junction where the red walk branches away to the left. Follow the yellow waymarkers to the right, go through a forestry gate and descend on the road back to the car park.

Kirstie's sacrifice is far from unique. These hills are covered with cairns marking the spot where other shepherds died. About ½ mile (800m) to the south west of Kirstie's Cairn a memorial can be found on the flank of Pinbreck Hill. That was where Kirstie's brother, Jimmy, died many years later.

> **WHAT TO LOOK FOR**   ⓘ
> A legend tells of a fight between the Laird of Changue and Auld Nick. Changue was short of cash and sold his soul to the Devil. When it was time to pay up he reneged, placed his Bible in front of him and drew a circle around him with his sword. The Devil let him be. You can see the circle and the **Devil's footprints** near the end of this walk

Discover Dunaskin Iron Works

A hill walk from a 19th-century industrial monument to a deserted, but not forgotten, village.

•DISTANCE•	4 miles (6.4km)
•MINIMUM TIME•	3hrs
•ASCENT / GRADIENT•	492ft (150m)
•LEVEL OF DIFFICULTY•	
•PATHS•	Old rail and tram beds and rough hillside
•LANDSCAPE•	Hill, moorland and industrial buildings
•SUGGESTED MAP•	aqua3 OS Explorer 327 Cumnock & Dalmellington
•START / FINISH•	Grid reference: NX 440084
•DOG FRIENDLINESS•	Keep on lead near sheep and at lambing time
•PARKING•	Dunaskin Open Air Museum
•PUBLIC TOILETS•	At visitor centre

BACKGROUND TO THE WALK

During the Industrial Revolution, iron was one of the great growth industries. In 1836 Henry Houldsworth, owner of a mill in Glasgow, diversified his business interests and created the Coltness Iron Works. Ten years later he and his son John brought the iron industry to the remote Doon Valley. Henry built his iron foundry on the site of Dunaskin farm and the early Victorian field pattern remains in outline surrounding the works.

New Industry

The area, although rich in iron, coal and water, was almost totally lacking in transport links. Everything for the construction of the foundry had to be brought in by train to Ayr and then by horse to Dunaskin. Twenty four pairs of horses were needed to haul the great beam for the blast engines alone. Iron was continually produced here from 1848 until 1921, when the buildings became a brickworks and then a processing plant for the coal mines until the late 1970s. One of the most complete Industrial Revolution ironworks in Europe, it has now been restored by a conservation trust and is open as a museum.

At the time the Dunaskin Iron Works were built, the principal industries of the area were agriculture and weaving and the population of the Upper Doon Valley was a mere 250 at Patna and a further 800 in the parish of Dalmellington. Skilled workers were brought in to provide the core of the workforce for the ironworks. They were joined by local men, leaving agricultural work in hope of higher wages, as well as tin miners from Cornwall, itinerant English workers and Highlanders displaced by the Clearances.

New Homes

The company built Waterside village opposite the ironworks to house the workers. High above on the Knockkippen plateau, twin villages were built close to the iron ore mines. The two villages of Lethanhill and Burnfoothill were considered as one, commonly known as the 'Hill, by the close-knit communities. Linked to the outside world by tram and railway lines this community survived the closure of the mines, the end of smelting at Dunaskin and two world wars. Ironically it was killed off by the post-war drive to improve housing.

Sanitation and overcrowding were a problem on the 'Hill and when the local authority decided to concentrate new building in nearby Patna and Dalmellington, the quality of the new housing was irresistible. No one wanted to leave but gradually the population dwindled until the last man, James Stevenson, departed on 31 August 1954. All that remains today are the bare outlines of houses among the trees, the war memorial with its poppy wreath still laid each Armistice Sunday and a simple stone painted white with the poignant inscription 'Long live the 'Hill 1851–1954'.

Walk 21

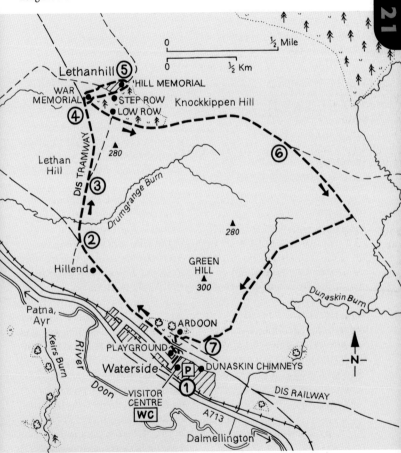

Walk 21 Directions

① Turn right in front of the **visitor centre** and follow the road towards the adventure playground. Go uphill on a track to the right of the playground and through woodland. Emerge at a T-junction opposite a

railway bridge and turn left on to a grassy trail.

② When you reach a metal gate across the trail, go through a small wooden one at its side. Climb over the next gate, turn right and head uphill following the line of a disused tramway, between the ends of an old bridge. This is the trackbed of the former horse-drawn tramway, which was used to bring the iron ore down from the plateau.

③ At the top of the hill, when the path divides, keep left and follow the path as it goes through two short sections of wall. The ground to your right in front of the conifer plantation was once the village football field. Where the path is blocked by a fence, turn right, then go left through a gate and right on to a metalled lane.

> **WHAT TO LOOK FOR** ℹ
> The **foundations** of the former church and schoolhouse can be seen on the ground behind the war memorial. The church was sold to a local silver band and was rebuilt in Dalmellington. Look also in the remains of the houses of **Low Row** for floral tributes hung on the trees by former residents who still walk here on a regular basis.

④ Head along here, past the remains of the miners' houses of **Step Row**, which are clearly visible amongst the trees. A stone **memorial** to the 'Hill stands near the site of the former village store. To the right of this, and now within the wood, is the former village square and the remains of more houses.

⑤ From the stone memorial turn back towards the war memorial, then return to the gate at the corner of the wood and continue along the

> **WHERE TO EAT AND DRINK** ℹ
> The child-friendly **Chimneys Restaurant**, which is part of the Dunaskin Open Air Museum, is a fairly basic sort of place but the friendly staff serve up a decent variety of good quality food and an excellent bowl of soup which is just the job on a cold day. When Chimneys is closed try one of the hotels in the centre of Dalmellington.

track beside the wood. In the trees are the remains of **Low Row**. Go Through another gate and continue along the former railway. When it forks, keep right.

⑥ Continue until the route ahead is blocked by sheets of corrugated iron, near a wall. Turn right and follow the line of the wall downhill. Cross a wall and continue walking downhill towards the chimneys of Dunaskin. When you reach a broken hedge, near the end of the **Green Hill**, turn right along the front of it and continue along here until you are level with the second of Dunaskin's chimneys.

⑦ Turn left here, heading downhill a short way and then though a gate. Veer to the right and head towards a wooded area. Go through the wood and emerge at **Ardoon**. Go past the house, turn left on to a footpath and follow it downhill and under a small, disused railway bridge. Cross the track and carry on heading back downhill on the footpath which leads back to the visitor centre.

> **WHILE YOU'RE THERE** ℹ
> Naturally a visit to the **Dunaskin Open Air Museum** should not be missed, it is open April–October, daily 10–5. Allow at least 2 hours for a visit and wear sturdy footwear and outdoor clothing. Just along the road, on the north edge of Dallmellington, is the **Scottish Industrial Railway Centre**, operated by enthusiasts from the Ayrshire Rail Preservation Group. This is as much part of the local story as the ironworks and every Sunday in July and August they offer trips on a working steam train.

On Old Roads and Rails Around Muirkirk

Walk around a once prosperous moorland town that stood at the crossroads of history.

•DISTANCE•	3½ miles (5.7km)
•MINIMUM TIME•	3hrs
•ASCENT / GRADIENT•	16ft (5m) ▲ ▲ ▲
•LEVEL OF DIFFICULTY•	🚶 🚶 🚶
•PATHS•	Old railway beds, farm tracks and country lanes, 1 stile
•LANDSCAPE•	Moorland, pastures and woodland
•SUGGESTED MAP•	aqua3 OS Explorer 328 Sanquhar & New Cumnock
•START / FINISH•	Grid reference: NX 696265
•DOG FRIENDLINESS•	Good, locals walk their dogs here
•PARKING•	Walkers' car park, Furnace Road
•PUBLIC TOILETS•	None on route

BACKGROUND TO THE WALK

In the early 17th century Muirkirk was little more than a crude little settlement called Garan on a dirt track that ran from Ayr to Edinburgh. The building of the Moor Kirk of Kyle led eventually to a name change to Muirkirk. An abundance of minerals such as coal, limestone and iron ore in the locality would inevitably make it a centre of industry and bring great prosperity.

'Tar' McAdam

Coal mining was well under way when John Loudon McAdam (1756–1836) came here in 1786 to set up a tar works. Known locally as 'Tar' McAdam, he would later go on to develop his famous method of road construction and this is where he carried out his first experiments. Furnace Road leading to the walkers' car park was used in his first trials and road surfaces are still referred to as tarmac today.

Iron and Coal

Muirkirk became the site of Ayrshire's first ironworks in 1787 when James Ewing & Co opened here. Three years later a canal had been dug to transport ore and coal on a series of barges from the Lightshaw, Auldhouseburn and Crossflat mines east of the works. Tram lines ran to the west and a series of bogie tracks led from the various pits to the canals. The Kames Colliery was opened in 1799 and would become the longest operating coal mine in the area. The canal was eventually replaced by the railway when the Glasgow and South Western Railway Company opened the Auckinleck-to-Muirkirk branch line in 1848. From this main line a maze of spur lines ran to the production areas.

Muirkirk had become a prosperous and thriving community. It was the first town in Britain to get gas lighting following the construction of the Muirkirk Coke & Gaslight Co in 1859. At its peak, the town had a population in excess of 5,000 with 1,000 employed in the ironworks alone.

Into Decline

But nothing lasts forever. Mines become exhausted, or seams run out and industrial trends change. The ironworks ceased production in 1923, following a strike by the workers. Iron ore mining had stopped some time previously and the ore was shipped in from further afield. During the strike the furnaces cooled with iron still inside them and rather than go to the expense of restoring them the company shut down.

The elaborate façade of the works which locals had dubbed 'The Castle' was demolished in 1968, the same year that the Kames Colliery finally closed. By this time the railway had disappeared under the axe of Dr Beeching in the mid-1960s. With no industry left the population drifted away and Muirkirk gradually declined to the small community that remains today.

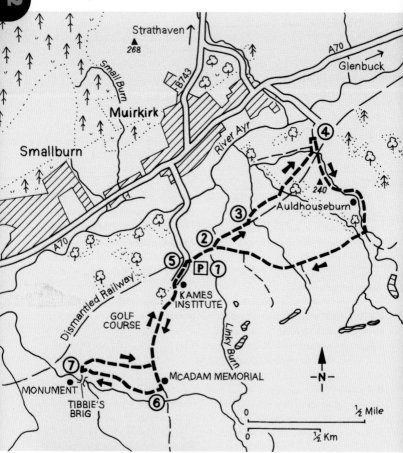

Walk 22 Directions

① From the car park follow the blue waymarker and exit via a gate on to a rough track with a high wall running along to the right. This continues as a fence and, once past the end of it, look for a waymarker pole on the left.

② Turn left on to a grass track. Follow this to some steps, go downhill and through a kissing gate. Turn right and walk along what may have been the bank of the 18th-century canal. Go through a kissing gate then veer left on to a rough track at the next waymarker.

③ Follow this to a duckboard and stile, cross here, turn left on to a short section of gravel path then turn right at a waymarker. The railway track here appears to fork. Keep to the left and continue along the trackbed eventually reaching a kissing gate.

WHERE TO EAT AND DRINK ℹ
There is a fish and chip shop in Muirkirk, otherwise try Cumnock, to the west, and enjoy a bar meal in any of the hotels or pubs on the main street or around the town centre.

④ Go through the gate and turn right on to the quiet country road. Follow this past the remains of an old railway bridge, past a farm entrance on the right then go through a gate to continue on a farm road. At the next gate turn right, go through four gates and return to the car park.

⑤ Turn right and exit the car park on to Furnace Road then turn left. Continue past the clock tower of the derelict Kames Institute and along the edge of a golf course. Go through a gate and continue, passing a cottage on the left, on to the old drove road to Sanquhar. Go through another gate and continue to the McAdam memorial.

⑥ Just past this head along a green track on the right. When it forks left on to what may have been a

WHAT TO LOOK FOR ℹ
No matter where you are on this walk there will be some signs of Muirkirk's former industrial prosperity. Look out for the grassed over beds of former bogie tracks, tramways, railway lines and the outline of the former canal bank. The sandstone building with the clock tower is the former Kames Institute once an important social facility and now derelict.

tramline keep right. Follow this track along the side of a stream until it joins a dirt track just above Tibbie's Brig. Near here, in a small clay dwelling lived a local poetess, Tibbie Pagan, who eked out a living by singing, selling her poetry and possibly supplying illicit whisky. She is believed locally to have been the source of the song *Ca the Yowes tae the Knowes* although Burns himself collected it from a clergyman. She published a volume of her poems in 1803.

⑦ Go down to the Brig and the monument then return uphill keeping left on the access for the disabled route to McAdam's cairn. Follow this back to the drove road where you turn left to return to the car park.

WHILE YOU'RE THERE ℹ
Head east on the A70 to the site of the former mining village of Glenbuck. Sadly it has now vanished under a mighty open-cast pit, but it was once the 'Nursery of Scottish Football' turning out a phenomenal number of professional players including the Shankley brothers – the most famous of whom was the legendary Bill who was born here in 1913. A memorial stands by the side of the road leading to Glenbuck.

Walk 23

Darvel Byways

In the footsteps of Sir Alexander Fleming, Darvel's most famous son, and the discovery of penicillin.

•DISTANCE•	7 miles (11.3km)
•MINIMUM TIME•	3hrs
•ASCENT / GRADIENT•	459ft (140m) ▲▲▲
•LEVEL OF DIFFICULTY•	🚶🚶🚶
•PATHS•	Country lanes and pavements
•LANDSCAPE•	Hillside, moorland, pasture and townscape
•SUGGESTED MAP•	aqua3 OS Explorer 334 East Kilbride, Galston & Darvel
•START / FINISH•	Grid reference: NX 563374
•DOG FRIENDLINESS•	Dogs fine on this walk
•PARKING•	On-street parking at Hastings Square at start of walk
•PUBLIC TOILETS•	None on route

BACKGROUND TO THE WALK

Lochfield Farm, the birthplace of Alexander Fleming (1881–1955), was the ideal childhood home for a boy with an insatiable curiosity about nature. Together with his brothers, the young Alexander spent much of his time roaming the moors identifying birds, animals and plants and guddling (catching by hand) trout in the nearby burns. He regarded his early education at Loudoun Moor School and later at Darvel as the foundation on which his later career was built.

Medical School

By the age of 13 he had moved to London to live with his brother Tom. Finishing his education at London Polytechnic, Fleming spent four years working as a clerk in a shipping office until the death of an uncle left him a small legacy which enabled him to take a short course of private tuition. He gained first place in the examination which would allow him to enter medical school. Fleming subsequently took first place in every exam he sat.

By 1906 Fleming had joined the Inoculation Department at St Mary's Hospital in Paddington and by 1909 was a Fellow of the Royal College of Surgeons. A period spent as a captain in the Army Medical Corps interrupted his career at St Mary's but after the war he returned there and by 1928 had become Professor of Bacteriology.

A Fortunate Discovery

That year, while clearing up some old virus cultures in his laboratory, Fleming noticed that although all were covered in moulds, one was significantly different. This particular mould was dissolving the virus colonies round about it and was spreading across the dish destroying the rest. The mould was one of a class called penicillium and, as Fleming afterwards stated, 'It was my good fortune that one particular penicillium blew on to a culture plate I was playing with.'

Discovering what we now know as penicillin was just the beginning. Isolating, extracting and finding a means of using it to treat infection would take another ten years and it was the 1940s before this 'magic bullet' was commercially available. Since then it has saved countless thousands of lives and a huge industry has grown round the research and development of other antibiotics. Honours were heaped upon Fleming. In 1944 he was knighted. The following year he was awarded the Nobel Prize for Medicine and on the 26 October 1946 he returned to his native Darvel to receive ' the proudest title I could have… the Freedom of Darvel.' Fleming spent the rest of his life working, lecturing and travelling. His last visit to Darvel was in June 1952 when he presented the Alexander Fleming Dux Medal and addressed the pupils at his old school. On 11 March 1955 Fleming died from a heart attack; he is buried in St Paul's Cathedral.

Walk 23 Directions

① From the **Alexander Fleming Memorial**, cross the square to the pedestrian crossing, cross the road, turn right and go along **Main Street**. Near the outskirts of the town cross **Darvel Bridge** and take the second turning on the left just past the **John Aird Factory**. Go uphill on this road and pass the cemetery.

② Keep going uphill to a crossroads near **New Quarterhouse farm**. Follow the waymark arrow pointing left. The road continues uphill, passing **Henryton** on the right and then **Byres** on the left. Near Byres

---

WHERE TO EAT AND DRINK ⓘ

Sitting at the foot of Loudoun Hill, with superb views of the surrounding countryside, is the **Loudounhill Inn**. This family-run establishment is friendly and warm with a good selection of beers and a full restaurant menu. It's just one mile (1.6km) east of Darvel on the A71 and has a real fire in the bar.

---

there is a conveniently situated bench by the roadside if you want some respite on this steep climb.

③ **Little Glen** is the next farm on the left-hand side and shortly afterwards the road forks. Take the left turn. The next two farms passed on this road are Meikleglen and Feoch which come in quick succession. Just before the next farm on the left, **Laigh Braidley**, a farm road leads off to the right. This is the entrance to Lochfield, Alexander Fleming's birthplace, which is not open to the public. Continue past Laigh Braidley.

④ After Laigh Braidley the road turns sharply left, then right and goes downhill to cross the **Glen Water** at Braidley Bridge. As you descend the hill look slightly to the right and uphill and you will see the steading of Lochfield, which is still farmed. Follow the road uphill from the bridge. There's another bench by the roadside at the T-junction near the top of the hill. Enjoy a

well-earned rest here and appreciate the splendid view back across the Irvine Valley.

⑤ Ignore the waymark and turn left, heading along a lane and past **Gateside**. When the road forks take the left fork, cross **Mucks Bridge** and continue uphill. The lane now passes the roads to Low then High Carlingcraig, then levels out. As you continue along the top of this hill look to the left for the distinctive outline of Loudoun Hill.

⑥ When you reach **Dyke** the road heads downhill again. Go over a crossroads at **Intax** and continue a short distance to some bungalows on the right. Just past here take a left turn. After **Hilltop** the road turns sharply right and downhill. As you approach the town the lane continues into **Burn Street**. At the T-junction turn left and follow this back to **Hastings Square**.

WHAT TO LOOK FOR ⓘ

Look out for the distinctive shape of **Loudoun Hill** to your right as you head uphill from the cemetery. This is the plug of an extinct volcano and the scene of several battles. William Wallace and a small party of men ambushed an English detachment here in 1297. Ten years later Robert the Bruce defeated an army three times the size of his own during the Scottish Wars of Independence (1286–1370).

WHILE YOU'RE THERE ⓘ

Loudoun Castle, one of the most impressive ruins in Scotland, was built in the early 19th century on the site of a previous keep. Known as the 'Windsor of Scotland' it was destroyed by fire on the night of 1 December 1941 and lay derelict for years. Now part of a huge theme park it is an ideal place for families with children. Nearby **Kilmarnock** was once the centre of the rail industry. Andrew Barclay's Victorian locomotive works built steam engines which were sent all over the world. Some are still in use today in countries such as India. The first steam passenger railway was the Kilmarnock-to-Troon line, which crossed the recently restored Laigh Milton viaduct, the oldest in Scotland. The first steam train ran on this line in 1816.

And on to Newmilns

A longer walk taking in the lace capital of Scotland.
See map and information panel for Walk 23

•DISTANCE•	11½ miles (18.5km)
•MINIMUM TIME•	6hrs
•ASCENT / GRADIENT•	98ft (30m) ▲ ▲ ▲
•LEVEL OF DIFFICULTY•	👫 👫 👫

Walk 24 Directions
(Walk 23 option)

The Irvine Valley was a major centre of handloom weaving for centuries. Huguenot and Flemish immigrants fleeing religious persecution in the 16th century, brought with them advanced skills including home lace making and the draw loom for pattern weaving.

At **Intax** (Point Ⓐ) turn right heading along a country lane passing **Cronan** on the left and the road to Brownhill on the right. Take a left turn where the road forks. The lane turns sharply right and then left as it passes **Dalwhatswood** then goes steeply downhill to enter the town of **Newmilns**.

By the end of the 18th century Newmilns had become the centre of the Ayrshire weaving industry. The quality of Irvine Valley weaving was further improved by Joseph Hood a talented and inspirational engineer and loom builder.

Follow this street to the T-junction then turn left and head along the **Main Street**. At **Criagview Road** turn right, go past the library, cross a bridge and turn left on to **Brown's**

Road to Darvel. A short distance along this road, near a lodge house and estate gates, go left on to a footpath and follow it along the banks of the river. The footpath ends near another lodge house and entrance gates to **Lanfine Estate**. Turn left here and cross **Randalcoup Bridge**. Continue along **Randalcoup Road**, with the park on your left, and look out for the splendid architecture of **Darvel Nursery School** also on the left.

At the T-junction cross **Main Street** and continue along **Cross Street**. Turn left at the T-junction and go along **West Donnington Street**, looking out for the old lace factories, some of which still produce lace today.

Alexander Morton purchased a lace curtain machine and Joseph Hood continued to improve the machinery in the lace factories. But, unable to compete with lace from Nottingham, the Irvine Valley went into decline. However, a revival of interest in traditional cotton lace, has brought new life to Darvel and Newmilns, where some 19th-century looms are still in operation.

At the junction with **Burn Street** (Point Ⓑ) turn left and continue back to **Hastings Square**.

Walk 25

The River Irvine Walk

The tragic tale of Lady Flora Hastings of Loudoun Castle.

•DISTANCE•	7½ miles (12.1km)
•MINIMUM TIME•	4hrs
•ASCENT / GRADIENT•	187ft (57m) ▲▲▲
•LEVEL OF DIFFICULTY•	🚶 🚶 🚶
•PATHS•	Pavements, footpaths and farm roads, 1 stile
•LANDSCAPE•	River valley, woodland and town
•SUGGESTED MAP•	aqua3 OS Explorer 334 East Kilbride, Galston & Darvel
•START / FINISH•	Grid reference: NS 539373
•DOG FRIENDLINESS•	Keep on lead near livestock
•PARKING•	On-street parking near Lady Flora's Institute in Newmilns
•PUBLIC TOILETS•	None on route

Walk 25 Directions

Lady Flora (1806–39) was the youngest daughter of the Marquis of Hastings and the Countess of Loudoun. She grew up at Loudoun Castle and then moved to London to be lady-in-waiting to Queen Victoria's mother, the Duchess of Kent. When Lady Flora complained of pains and swelling of her abdomen, she was examined by the royal physician, Sir James Clark, who was unable to diagnose the cause. Rumours circulated that Lady Flora was pregnant and she was ostracised at Court and shunned by Victoria, despite an intimate examination by two

doctors proving that she could not possibly be pregnant. Whether the rumours were started by Victoria or Sir James Clark is not known, but Clark continued in his post and the Queen made no attempt to protect Lady Flora from gossip.

Flora's uncle published a detailed account of the sorry affair in a newspaper and public opinion was with Lady Flora, who was cheered wherever she went. This was in stark contrast to the public's treatment of Victoria, who was booed on the streets of London.

When Flora died, a post mortem revealed an enlarged liver. Bad feeling towards the Queen came to a head at the funeral procession. Following the coffin, a line of empty coaches, including the empty state coach of the young Queen, represented the highest families in the land. The crowds stoned the Queen's empty carriage to the cry of 'murderer'. Lady Flora's body was taken to Loudoun Castle and from there to the family vault at Loudoun Kirk.

WHERE TO EAT AND DRINK ⓘ

The **Wee Train** at 22 Wallace Street in Galston is an old-fashioned pub with the atmosphere of a bygone age. A roaring log fire in the bar provides warmth and comfort while you wait for the food. On the menu are some traditional Scottish favourites like steak pie and braised steak and on a cold or windy day you can't beat the home-made soup.

Walk 25

Start the walk from **Lady Flora's Institute**, a girls' school which opened shortly after her death. Built with the proceeds of a book of her poetry, it was a fitting memorial to a poplar local woman.

Walk along **Main Street** and turn left into **Craigview Road**. Cross a bridge, turn right and follow this road to the T-junction. Turn left and continue along this road. At the fork keep right, go along the side of a factory building then turn left into **Stonygate Road** and keep on it to join the **River Irvine Footpath**. Stroll along this path by the riverside passing Strath then, at the dog kennels, follow a diversion around the buildings. The walkway continues from here as a well-defined, if muddy, path.

Go through woodlands, continuing along the river bank. When a white cottage comes into view and the track forks, go left. Go through a gap stile and take the surfaced road to the left of **Barr Mill**, uphill to join a main road. Follow this road downhill passing the library, social club and the Masonic Arms to the junction at the **Four Corners**.

Turn right then cross the road and continue out of town crossing the **Muckle Brig** and then, at a roundabout, cross the Galston bypass to continue on the pavement beside the **A719**. Pass **Waterside Farm** and **Loudoun Academy** before reaching the entrance gates to **Loudoun Castle**.

Turn left and follow the lane for approximately ½ mile (800m) to **Loudoun Kirk Bridge** then turn left and enter the kirkyard to visit the Loudoun family vault. Leaving the kirkyard, cross a small bridge. Turn

right on to the signposted Galston footpath. After 100yds (91m) the path bends to the right. Go straight ahead on to a grassy footpath.

Follow this well-defined track to its junction with the Galston bypass and turn right, crossing a bridge then heading downhill to the right. Turn left at a waymarker and go through the underpass to the other side of the bypass. Turn left and follow the well-defined track along the river bank.

WHAT TO LOOK FOR

In Galston look out for the red-brick dome of the Catholic **Church of St Sophia**. This Victorian building was modeled on the Byzantine Agia Sophia in Istanbul and has long dominated the skyline of this former mining town. Although closed it has recently received a grant and is to be restored.

At the end of this path turn right into a narrow lane and, at its junction with **Titchfield Street**, turn left. At the next T-junction turn right, cross the road, follow it round the corner and take the first turning on the left. Continue past two school buildings and a cemetery to a staggered junction.

Cross the **B7037** and continue along **Clockstone Road** which heads away to the right. At the T-junction go left then take the next right turn beside a house, go past some houses then downhill. Ascend again, to **Piersland Farm** and a grand view of the Irvine Valley.

Head back downhill on this farm road, cross a gate where the road turns sharply left and then go under a railway bridge. Turn right and retrace your route along **Stonygate Road** back to the start.

The Museum of Scottish Country Life

An 18th-century time warp in a late 20th-century new town.

•DISTANCE•	5 miles (8km)
•MINIMUM TIME•	3hrs
•ASCENT / GRADIENT•	262ft (80m) ▲▲▲
•LEVEL OF DIFFICULTY•	🚶 🚶 🚶
•PATHS•	Farm tracks and country roads
•LANDSCAPE•	Pastureland, woodland and new town
•SUGGESTED MAP•	aqua3 OS Explorer 342 Glasgow
•START / FINISH•	Grid reference: NS 608558
•DOG FRIENDLINESS•	Keep on lead near livestock
•PARKING•	Car park at Museum of Scottish Country Life
•PUBLIC TOILETS•	At museum

BACKGROUND TO THE WALK

On the outskirts of East Kilbride, Scotland's largest and busiest new town, Wester Kittochside farm sits in a time warp. Preserved as the Museum of Scottish Country Life, it is still a working farm but without any of the high-tech machinery of 21st century farming – its clock has stopped in the 1950s.

John Reid

In 1567 John Reid, the tenant of Kittochside, bought land from Robert Muir of Caldwell. Muir tried to retake the land by force some 20 years later, attacking the farm 'armed with spears, swords and other fearful wapponis.' Reid was threatened, his possessions seized and his house burned. But the matter was adjudicated by the Privy Council, which found for Reid and ordered Muir to pay compensation.

'Modern' Farming Methods

The agrarian revolution to modernise and industrialise farming was enthusiastically embraced in the 1780s by Reid's descendant, another John. He transformed his two patches of arable land and his sheep grazed the moorland. New fields were laid out and enclosed, drainage was installed to improve the ground and boundary hedges were created. Reid introduced crop rotation, new crops, including turnips and grass for winter feed, and changed the stock emphasis to cattle. By the time he was finished, most of the old buildings on the farm had gone, replaced by the new steading that stands today.

The Reid family continued to farm at Wester Kittochside. A dairy and barn were built in the latter half of the 19th century and a threshing mill and horse 'gin' (engine – a large wheel turned by horse power to run machinery) were installed.

Time Stands Still

In 1963 dairy production ceased and the land switched to grazing beef cattle. James Reid, the tenth generation to farm here, never carried out any improvements or modernised his farming in any way and for a period of 50 years Wester Kittochside never changed. Reid continued to farm as his father had, so no grain driers, huge silos, slurry tanks or modern cattle units were installed.

James Reid and his wife had no children and gifted the farm to the National Trust for Scotland. James died in 1982 and Margaret, his wife, carried on until 1992 when she left the house ending nearly four centuries occupation by a single family. Since the farm opened to the public as a museum, the dairy has been reinstated and the land is farmed as it was in 1950, including the five to six shift crop rotation and grazing supporting milk cattle and working horses. Crops of grass, hay and turnips are still used for winter feed. The techniques and equipment evoke memories of a way of life that has long past, except here at Wester Kittochside farm.

Walk 26 Directions

① Exit the car park and turn right on to the road, heading past the front of the main **Exhibition Building** then turn right on to a farm road. Continue along this, keeping an eye open for the tractors ferrying visitors from the Exhibition Building to the farm. Take a gated turn off to the left and follow this path to go through another gate on to a farm road.

Walk 26

WHERE TO EAT AND DRINK ⓘ

The museum Exhibition Building contains an excellent child-friendly **café** where visitors can enjoy hot soup, sandwiches, snacks and wonderfully fattening sweet and sticky things. Alternatively go into East Kilbride and seek out the heart of the old village and try the bar meals in the 18th-century **Montgomery Arms**, the oldest pub in the area.

② Turn left and, a short distance further on, turn right, on to another farm road. Follow this across a field and into the wooded area surrounding **Wester Kittochside**. The road turns sharply right then joins another road. Turn left, walk past a bungalow then turn left again where the farm road joins a country road.

③ Follow this quiet road for just over a mile (1.6km), past some of the fields of Wester Kittochside farm, then the fields of more modern farms and finally into the village of **Carmunnock**. The road ends at a T-junction. Turn right then, a short distance further on, take the next turning on the right into **Cathkin Road**.

④ Keep on Cathkin Road for about ½ mile (800m) then, when it bends sharply to the left, turn right and continue straight ahead on a minor road. Follow this as it twists and turns to reach **Highflat Farm** after about ½ mile (800m) and then continues for another ½ mile (800m) to end at a T-junction opposite the road leading to **West Rogerton farm**.

⑤ Turn right and, in just over ½ mile (800m), you will come to a crossroads. On the right is a farm track leading back to **Highflat**. Turn left here and proceed to the next T-junction. Walk along this country lane passing the farm of **East Kittochside** on the left.

⑥ Pass a junction on the right, continue through **Kittochside**, pass the drive to **Kittochside House** and reach another T-junction. Cross the road here and continue along the farm track ahead of you. Take the first turning on the left on to another farm track and, at the end of this, you will be back in front of the museum **Exhibition Building**.

WHAT TO LOOK FOR ⓘ

The fields at Wester Kittochside remain unaltered since the middle of last century in marked contrast to those of the surrounding farms. Compare the **hedgerows** and fields of Wester Kittochside with those of other farms like Highflat to see the differences in fencing arrangements and the abundance and variety of wild flowers growing on each.

WHILE YOU'RE THERE ⓘ

The **Museum of Scottish Country Life** is one of the most important and entertaining attractions to have opened in Scotland for decades. The main Exhibition Building has a comprehensive collection covering the entire history of Scottish farming. However, it is the farm steading and the magnificent Georgian farmhouse, unchanged in the last half century and little changed since the 18th century that turns an interesting visit to a magical experience. Open all year daily, 10–5.

The Spectacular Falls at Glenashdale

Enjoy this short scenic woodland walk over the Isle of Arran's ancient bedrock.

•DISTANCE•	2¾ miles (4.4km)
•MINIMUM TIME•	2hrs
•ASCENT / GRADIENT•	442ft (135m) ▲▲▲
•LEVEL OF DIFFICULTY•	🏃🏃🏃
•PATHS•	Forest paths and forest roads
•LANDSCAPE•	Woodland, waterfalls, rock
•SUGGESTED MAP•	aqua3 OS Explorer 361 Isle of Arran
•START / FINISH•	Grid reference: NS 047252
•DOG FRIENDLINESS•	Good, locals walk their dogs here
•PARKING•	Car park opposite youth hostel in Whiting Bay
•PUBLIC TOILETS•	None on route; nearest at Shore Road, Whiting Bay

BACKGROUND TO THE WALK

Millions of years ago this area was a hot and barren desert. During what geologists refer to as the Permian period, 270 million years ago, the underlying red sandstone gradually formed from sand dunes. On top of this a sill (layer) of igneous rocks was laid down in the Tertiary period 210 million years later.

The Glenashdale Sill
The Tertiary sill at Glenashdale is about 100ft (30m) thick and composed of several types of igneous rock, the major part being quartz-dolerite. When this is harder than the surrounding rock, it stands proud as the softer rocks are eroded. At Glenashdale continual erosion has created these spectacular waterfalls and, where the stream and the waterfall have cut into the Glenashdale sill, it is easy to examine the now exposed structure of the rocks. Following the stream up from the waterfall the banks and bed of the stream reveal the dark and medium grained igneous rocks with a few specks of pyrites – a shiny yellow mineral. South west of the falls there are veins of a dark basalt. Pack one of those small geological field guides in your backpack, or in a pocket, and use the photographs to help identify the various different kinds of rock found on the route.

Native and Exotic Trees
A field guide to trees could also prove useful although several of the trees have been conveniently labelled. There is an abundance of native trees like the alder, hazel, downy birch, oak, ash and rowan. The latter, also called the mountain ash, has bright red berries in the autumn and in Scottish folklore was used for warding off witches.

You'll also find a wide variety of unusual and exotic trees in the glen. The Siberian crab has white flowers and small green berries which may eventually turn into bright red fruits. You'll also come across large specimens of the Douglas fir. This evergreen native of North America is extensively planted in Europe to provide high grade timber but seldom reaches its maximum height of 328ft (100m). Most European specimens tend to be around 180ft (55m). Other North American species include the Great fir and the Sitka spruce. This fast growing conifer often reaches heights of 197ft (60m) and although it thrives in a range of soils, it is particularly suited to the mild, wet Scottish climate.

Growing on the edge of the path you'll find the heart shaped leaves of wood sorrel with its long stalked, white, bell-like flowers during April and May. There's a profusion of red campion and the scent of wild honeysuckle and pungent wild garlic mingle with the pine tang of the wood. If you look really hard you may even find a yellow pimpernel, with its star-like flowers, in May and August.

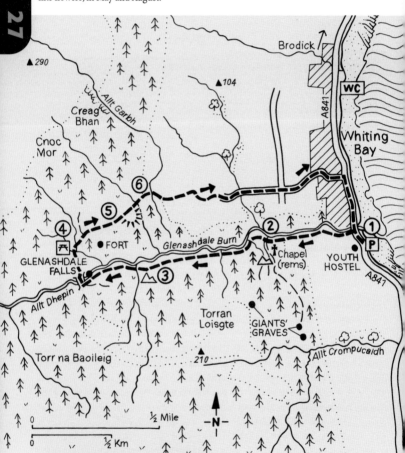

Walk 27 Directions

① From the car park turn right on to the road, cross it and turn left on to the footpath, signposted 'Giants' Graves and Glenashdale Falls'. Follow this leafy lane until it reaches the rear of a house, then continue on the path along the riverbank. Go through a gate, pass a forest walks sign and continue until you reach a signpost pointing in the direction of the **Giants' Graves**.

② The path forks here. Go right, following the sign to **Glenashdale Falls**. The path continues, rising

Walk 27

gently, through a wooded area, where several of the trees are identified by small labels fixed to the trunks. Continue uphill on this path, which is marked by the occasional waymarker, crossing several bridges and fording a shallow section of the burn.

③ Eventually the path starts to climb steeply uphill and continues to some steps and then forks. Keep right and follow this path to reach the falls. Keep on the path past the falls and continue uphill to cross a bridge. A picnic table situated on the riverbank here is a good spot to stop for refreshment.

> ### WHERE TO EAT AND DRINK ⓘ
> There are plenty of choices for eating and drinking in Whiting Bay. **The Pantry** on Shore Road is open every day until 9PM in the summer, with restricted hours from November. The **Trafalgar Restaurant**, also on Shore Road, serves a variety of main meals and snacks while the **Drift Inn**, just off Shore Road by Murchies, does superb bar food.

④ From here follow the path into an area planted with Sitka spruce. Keep to the track marked by the green waymarkers as it heads through this dark part, going through a gap in a wall and eventually arriving at a sign pointing to an **Iron-Age fort**. Turn off to look at the remains of the ramparts then retrace your steps to the sign and continue on the path.

> ### WHAT TO LOOK FOR ⓘ
> If you turn left at the sign for the Giants' Graves you can see the remains of **Whiting Bay Chapel**. In 20yds (18m) on the left look for a raised area covered with vegetation and poke about at the far end. Little remains but you should find some small gravestones.

⑤ Cross a bridge by another waterfall then follow more waymarkers to a clearing and a viewpoint. Sit on the bench here and enjoy the panoramic view across the wooded glen. From here you can see the full extent of the Glenashdale Falls as the water cascades over the top. A waymarker points uphill through a densely wooded area before ending at a T-junction with a forest road.

> ### WHILE YOU'RE THERE ⓘ
> Visit the **Giants' Graves**, an important neolithic site containing several chambered burial cairns of the kind found throughout Arran. Because of their semi-circular forecourts they have been called 'horned gallery graves'. The path to the graves is short but steep, climbing some 173 steps.

⑥ Turn right on to the forest road and continue, crossing water at a ford and going through three kissing gates until the route continues as a metalled road. Continue along this, go over a crossroads and wind downhill. Turn right at a T-junction and walk 200yds (183m) back to the car park.

Machrie Moor

Discover the standing stones of one of Scotland's finest early settlements on the Isle of Arran.

•DISTANCE•	5½ miles (8.8km)
•MINIMUM TIME•	3hrs
•ASCENT / GRADIENT•	114ft (35m) ▲ ▲ ▲
•LEVEL OF DIFFICULTY•	🚶🚶 🚶🚶 🚶🚶
•PATHS•	Footpaths, rough tracks, road, 3 stiles
•LANDSCAPE•	Forest, seashore, fields and moorland
•SUGGESTED MAP•	aqua3 OS Explorer 361 Isle of Arran
•START / FINISH•	Grid reference: NS 898314
•DOG FRIENDLINESS•	Keep on lead near livestock and where requested by signs
•PARKING•	King's Cave car park
•PUBLIC TOILETS•	Car park at Blackwaterfoot

BACKGROUND TO THE WALK

Arran is world famous for its archaeological remains dating from the mesolithic period. The island is littered with them, but the greatest concentration can be found on the wild, windswept Machrie Moor. For it was here that humans settled from the earliest of times and have left the remains of their hut circles, chambered cairns and standing stones. The circles of grey granite boulders and tall, weathered red sandstone pillars are an impressive sight against a winter sun on the wide expanse of moor.

Magnificent Monuments

The earliest inhabitants settled here some 8,000 years ago and, across the millennia, later settlements were created and the first simple monuments erected. Within this small area of moor there are over 40 stone circles, standing stones, chambered tombs and hut circles making it the finest neolithic and Bronze-Age site in Scotland. Most visitors head straight for the three large red sandstone pillars, the tallest of which stands slightly over 18ft (5.5m). These stones were once part of a much larger circle, the other stones have fallen or been removed. No one is absolutely certain what function these Bronze-Age circles performed, but it is likely that they had a religious significance. Many stone circles are precisely aligned to particular celestial events like the rising of the midsummer sun, and they possibly also fulfilled seasonal functions, indicating when to carry out certain rituals or to plant and harvest crops. A survey of the area by the archaeologist John Barnatt in 1978 revealed that four of the circles were aligned with a gap in the skyline of Machrie Glen, where the sun rises at midsummer.

Legendary Figures

Other early Arran inhabitants had another explanation for the circles. At a time when people attributed anything they did not understand to legendary figures the standing stones on Machrie Moor became the province of the giant Fingal, a Scottish form of the Irish warrior Finn MacCumhail and the double circle still has the name of Fingal's Cauldron Seat. According to legend Fingal put his dog Bran in the outer circle and tied it to a stone with a hole in it to stop it wandering while Fingal had his meal in the inner circle. The dwellers on the moor lived in round huts, the remains of which are still visible. There is no explanation as to why and when they departed, leaving their monuments, but one theory is that climate change forced them to move to a warmer and more sheltered part of the island. In the thousands of years since they left, the area has become covered by a blanket of peat bog. There is undoubtedly more to discover under this protective layer as recent excavations continue to uncover even older structures.

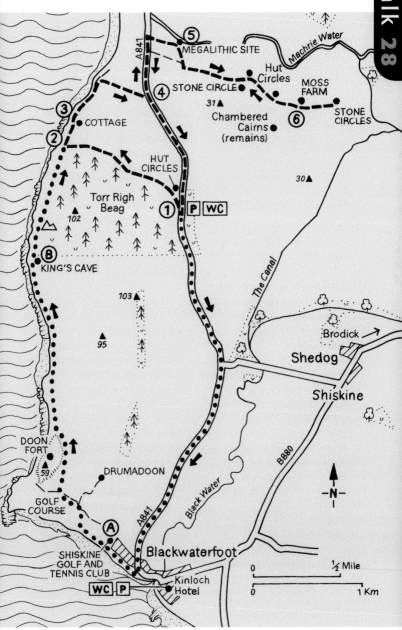

Walk 28 Directions

① From the car park take the footpath signposted for King's Cave. This goes through an area of woodland, past the site of some hut circles on the right and continues along the edge of the woods until it starts to head downhill towards the sea. Look out for a waymarker on the right pointing back in the direction you have just walked.

WHILE YOU'RE THERE   ⓘ

A little to the north of Machrie Moor, overlooking Machrie Bay is **Auchengallon Stone Circle**. Thought to be a Bronze-Age kerbed cairn, it once had a continuous kerb of sandstone blocks around its edge, and is 3,000 to 4,000 years old. Many of the blocks are now missing, but what remains is a spectacular stone circle enclosing a burial cairn, the finest burial site on the island.

---

② Turn right here on to a faint path, which in the summer will be very overgrown with bracken. Plough your way through this and, in a short distance, you will come to a wire fence, which you can easily climb through. Cross this field and go through a gate then head downhill aiming for the left end of a white **cottage** by the shore.

③ As you near the end of the cottage you will see a gate at the corner of the garden wall. Turn

---

WHAT TO LOOK FOR   ⓘ

Look for evidence of **hut circles** and **chambered tombs** as you walk along the road to the standing stones. There are two hut circles to the left of the path after it curves first left and then right and just before it meets a wall. Over this wall and about half-way to the next one there is a chambered cairn on the left.

---

right at the gate and follow the line of the fence on your right until you reach a stile. Cross the stile and turn left on to a farm road running between two fences. Keep on this road passing another cottage on the right and keeping right at the fork.

④ When the road ends at a T-junction with the **A841** turn left. Continue to the signpost for Machrie Moor Standing Stones. Turn right, go over a stile and follow the access road. This rough track passes through two fields.

WHERE TO EAT AND DRINK   ⓘ

Situated at the edge of the car park at Blackwaterfoot and overlooking the beach, the family-friendly **Kinloch Hotel** is the the best pit stop in this walk. The bar and restaurant meals are of a very high quality and served by friendly staff. Seafood is a speciality, with imaginative offerings like monkfish wrapped in smoked salmon served with fresh asparagus on a shellfish essence.

---

⑤ In the second field, near the far left-hand corner, is a megalithic site, one of the oldest in the area. Nothing is to be seen above ground, the site was only identified when flints were found that were around 7,000 to 9,000 years old. Continue on the road to the **Moss Farm Road stone circle**. Dating from approximately 2000 BC it has never been excavated.

⑥ From here the track continues, passing the deserted **Moss Farm** then crossing a stile to the main **stone circles** of Machrie Moor. When you have finished wandering around them return to the stile and take the **Moss Farm road** back to the **A841**. Turn left on to this and walk for approximately 1½ miles (2km) to return to the car park.

Robert the Bruce

Discover strange geological formations and the cave of a king.
See map and information panel for Walk 28

•DISTANCE•	5½ miles (8.8km)
•MINIMUM TIME•	2hrs 30min
•ASCENT / GRADIENT•	114ft (35m) ▲▲▲
•LEVEL OF DIFFICULTY•	🚶🚶 🚶

Walk 29 Directions (Walk 28 option)

From Point ① continue past the King's Cave car park and walk a further 2¼ miles (3.6km) to **Blackwaterfoot**. When the road curves to the left turn right and head towards **Shiskine Golf and Tennis Club** (Point Ⓐ). Go through the private car park and past the clubhouse on to a hard surfaced dirt road running parallel to the beach. Follow this as it turns right then forks left to reach gateposts at the drive to **Drumadoon farm**. Keep left following the signs for King's Cave. Soon another sign points to a path going uphill to the left to King's Cave. Follow this to a gate, cross the stile and continue on a faint path across fields, behind **Doon Fort**.

This is an Iron-Age fort thought to be about 2,000 years old. You can detour to it by following the signs before leaving the golf course.

Go through a kissing gate and continue on the track. Eventually reach a waymarker pointing downhill and follow the narrow twisting track downhill and then left as it continues parallel to the beach through bracken. From here looking back along the beach you have the best view of the sill on Doon Fort. Huge hexagonal columns, like those found on Staffa in west Scotland, or at the Giant's Causeway on the north coast of Northern Ireland, run the full length of the hill.

This well-trodden path continues in this direction to reach the **King's Cave** (Point Ⓑ). The caves get their name from Robert the Bruce who allegedly hid here for a time during the Scottish Wars of Independence. Whether this is the cave where he encountered the spider is not known, nor is it even certain that he ever did use it. Early humans did though and important archaeological remains have been found there. The caves are fronted by iron bars and kept locked to avoid damage to the interior.

Continue past the caves and follow the shoreline until the path heads uphill on a very steep and badly eroded surface. At the top of this section go over a stile and continue uphill on a rocky path. This will come into the open above the beach (Point ②). Continue on Walk 28 now or turn right here and keep on this path to return to the car park (Point ①).

Glasgow's Architecture

From the heart of the Merchant City to where it all started in the Old Town.

Walk 30

•DISTANCE•	2½ miles (4km)
•MINIMUM TIME•	3hrs
•ASCENT / GRADIENT•	82ft (25m)
•LEVEL OF DIFFICULTY•	
•PATHS•	City pavements
•LANDSCAPE•	City
•SUGGESTED MAP•	AA Street by Street Glasgow
•START / FINISH•	Grid reference: NS 592657
•DOG FRIENDLINESS•	Not best of walks for dogs
•PARKING•	Meters on street bays, multi-story in Sauchiehall Street
•PUBLIC TOILETS•	Queen Street Station

Walk 30 Directions

From the tourist office in **George Square** turn left into **Queen Street** and cross the road to the **Gallery of Modern Art**. This was built as the residence of William Cunninghame, a tobacco lord, in 1778 and is the finest of these mansions in the city. Later it became the Royal Exchange.

Exit the museum and cross to **Ingram Street** continuing along past the imposing façade of the Corinthian, formerly the Union Bank now housing the most ornate pub in the city. Turn right into **Virginia Place** and continue through to **Virginia Street**. Like the rest of the Merchant City the buildings here were built from the profits from the tobacco and sugar trade. At No 51 is Virginia Court where the tobacco merchants were based from 1817. Later it became the home of Jacobean Corsetry and although that company has long since departed their sign has been preserved on the wall. Nos 32–35 were the former Tobacco Exchange

then the Sugar Exchange, and are now being converted to apartments. Running parallel to this street is Miller Street where at No 42 is the Tobacco Merchants House, built in 1775, recently renovated and now housing offices.

From Virginia Street turn left into **Trongate**, left into **Hutcheson Street** then left again, back into **Ingram Street**. The white square building with the spire opposite here is Hutchesons' Hall built in 1805 on the site of a previous hospice built by George and Thomas Hutcheson. It now belongs to the National Trust for Scotland. Continue along **Ingram Street** to St David's parish church, more

WHERE TO EAT AND DRINK

Glasgow is the restaurant capital of Scotland and the only difficulty discerning diners have is making a choice. On this walk however its easy, for the **Cathedral House Restaurant** in Cathedral Square is an absolute gem of a place. French cuisine with a Scottish twist is the order of the day. Try the black pudding salad or the Toulouse sausage on mustard mash.

often referred to as the Ramshorn Church because of the legend of St Mungo turning a stolen ram's head into stone on this spot. It is now a theatre facility for Strathclyde University.

Continue along Ingram Street then, at the junction, turn left into **High Street** and proceed uphill. Pass **Cathedral Square Gardens** on the right, with an equestrian statue of William III, dressed as a Roman emperor. This is 'King Billy' the Dutch-born British monarch still revered by members of the Orange Lodge in Scotland and beyond for defeating the forces of the Stuart kings in the 17th century. The tail of the horse is supposed to move in the wind as it has an ingenious ball and socket joint.

WHILE YOU'RE THERE
The **Lighthouse** in Mitchell Lane, near Buchanan Street is one of Europe's largest architecture and design centres and it also contains the Charles Rennie Mackintosh Interpretation Centre. The renovated building, designed by Mackintosh, was previously the home of the *Glasgow Herald* newspaper.

Next to the gardens is the St Mungo Museum of Religious Life and Art, where Salvador Dali's controversial *Christ of St John of the Cross* is on display. This painting caused deep consternation among the prudent citizens of Glasgow, when it was purchased in 1952 for the then enormous sum of £8,200. Across the High Street from here is Glasgow's oldest house, **Provand's Lordship**. Built around 1471 for the priest in charge of the St Nicholas Hospital, it later became the house of the Canon of Barlanark, who was rector of the Lordship of Provan. Throughout its long history the

house has had many uses but somehow survived development to become a museum. Opposite Provand's Lordship is **Glasgow Cathedral**, a medieval building occupying a site of previous places of worship dating back to the founding of Glasgow, when St Mungo first established his cell beside the Molendinar Burn in the 6th century AD. A fine example of medieval Scottish architecture, it is the only mainland cathedral to have emerged intact from the Reformation. Deep within the building, which is more ornate than its stark exterior would suggest, is the tomb of St Mungo surrounded by four columns supporting fan vaulting. High on a hill behind the cathedral a statue of John Knox glowers down from his pedestal in Glasgow Necropolis, one of the great 19th-century cemeteries.

From Provand's Lordship turn left into **Cathedral Street**. Turn left again at the junction with **Montrose Street** and then right into **George Street** and back to **George Square**. Finish the walk by having a look at the rich ornamentation of the City Chambers, which dominates one end of the square. Built by the Victorian city fathers as a symbol of Glasgow's wealth and prosperity, it is still the municipal headquarters. Its exotic marble interior often moonlights as a film location.

WHAT TO LOOK FOR
Just north of the Cathedral Precinct is a pedestrian bridge that goes across the busy road to reach a large red sandstone school. This is the **Martyrs' Public School**, a traditional Glasgow public school but with one important difference. This one was designed by Charles Rennie Mackintosh.

Walk 31

Alexander 'Greek' Thomson

Discover a Victorian city and the architect who shaped it.

•DISTANCE•	6½ miles (10.4km)
•MINIMUM TIME•	3hrs 30min
•ASCENT / GRADIENT•	98ft (30m) ▲▲▲
•LEVEL OF DIFFICULTY•	𝕏 𝕏 𝕏
•PATHS•	Pavements
•LANDSCAPE•	City
•SUGGESTED MAP•	aqua3 OS Explorer 342 Glasgow; AA Street by Street
•START / FINISH•	Grid reference: NS 587653
•DOG FRIENDLINESS•	Not great walk for dogs
•PARKING•	Sauchiehall Street multi-storey or on-street parking
•PUBLIC TOILETS•	At Central Station

BACKGROUND TO THE WALK

More than any other architect Alexander Thomson was responsible for the shaping of Victorian Glasgow with his innovative use and interpretation of classical Greek designs. Born in 1817, in the Stirlingshire village of Balfron, he moved to Glasgow to live with an older brother. He was apprenticed to an architect and began studying the plans, drawings and engravings of classical architecture. This influence dominated his later style and earned him the nickname 'Greek' Thomson although he never travelled abroad.

Classical Influences

The range of his buildings was extraordinary, from churches to villas, warehouses, tenements and even a set of steps. Much of his work was destroyed by German bombing during World War Two and even more disappeared in the relentless modernisation of Glasgow during the 1960s and 70s. However, those buildings that have survived provide a fine cross section of his work. His one remaining church (1857–9) on St Vincent Street is a remarkable building with Grecian columns and an imposing tower, built on the side of Blythswood Hill. Near by, in Union Street, the curiously named Egyptian Halls (1871–3), an enormous stone fronted building with an interior constructed from cast iron, started life as an early form of shopping centre or bazaar. In the West End, near the Botanic Gardens, Thomson created the Great Western Terrace (1869), the 'grandest terrace in Glasgow' and took the unusual step of placing the tallest buildings in the middle of the row, rather than at the ends, which was more conventional at the time.

Another example of his terraces, Moray Place (1858), conveniently situated near the Cathcart Circle railway line, is where Thomson took up permanent residence. His home at No 1 is now the contact address for the Alexander Thomson Society and, like most of the houses he designed, is in private ownership.

One exception is Holmwood House (1858) in Cathcart, 4¹/₂ miles (7.2km) from the city centre, now owned by the National Trust for Scotland. Built for a wealthy paper manufacturer, it is an asymmetrical villa with a bay window, which looks like a Greek temple attached to the front of the building. It is probably Thomson's finest work and is now undergoing complete restoration.

Alexander Thomson Society

Although he gained prominence during his lifetime and was a major influence on later architects such as Charles Rennie Mackintosh and Frank Lloyd Wright, Thomson is little known today. Records of his work are limited to a few drawings held in Glasgow's Mitchell Library. His own office archive has vanished without a trace and were it not for the work of the Alexander Thomson Society, he would have remained in obscurity. However after much campaigning to preserve his remaining 24 buildings within the city and the publication of a book about the man, Thomson is beginning to regain the recognition he deserves.

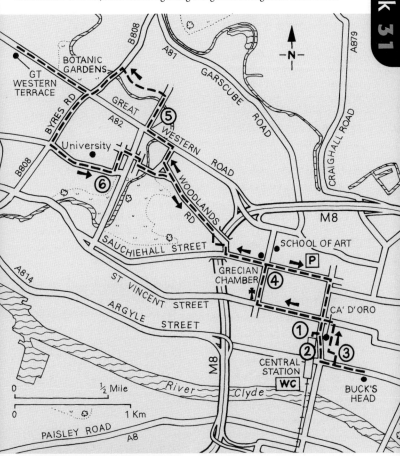

Walk 31 Directions

① Exit **Central Station** and turn right. At the junction with **Union Street** turn right. The building on the opposite corner is the **Ca' d'Oro** building, a late 19th-century Italianate warehouse by John Honeyman, based on the Golden House in Venice. The upper storeys are made of cast iron. A little way down Union Street from here on the same side as the Ca' d'Oro is Thomson's Egyptian Halls, sadly in need of some renovation.

② Cross over then head down Union Street turning left into **Argyll Street** at the next junction.

Cross Argyll Street then walk along to the junction with **Dunlop Street** where you will find the **Buck's Head** building, named after an inn previously on this spot. Cross Argyll Street again, retrace your steps, turning right into **Buchanan Street**. Turn left into **Mitchell Lane**, pass the Lighthouse (➤ While You're There, Walk 30), turn right.

③ Walk up Mitchell Street, continue along **West Nile Street** then turn left into **St Vincent Street**. Continue on this for just under ½ mile (800m), going uphill to the junction with **Pitt Street**. You are now standing in front of 'Greek' Thomson's St Vincent Street church, one of his greatest achievements. Cross St Vincent Street here then head up **Pitt Street** to **Sauchiehall Street**.

④ On the opposite corner is Thomson's **Grecian Chamber** (1865) and to the right along Scott Street is Rennie Mackintosh's Glasgow School of Art. From the front of the Grecian Chamber turn left, head down Sauchiehall Street to **Charing Cross** then take the pedestrian bridge over the motorway to **Woodlands Road**. Go along here until it ends at **Park Road**, turn right, then left again into **Great Western Road**.

WHERE TO EAT AND DRINK ⓘ

On a tour of Glasgow's architecture there can be only one place to dine. The **Willow Tearoom** in Sauchiehall Street was designed by Charles Rennie Mackintosh for Kate Cranston who had a string of tea rooms. Entered through a jeweller's shop, there is always a queue for the 1904, Room de Luxe, where everything including the chairs and tables are Mackintosh. It's worth the wait and the food is good and reasonably priced.

WHILE YOU'RE THERE ⓘ

Thomson designed **Holmwood House** in Cathcart for James Couper a paper manufacturer and everything including the interior design and the furniture came from Thomson's drawing board. Unfortunately the furniture has not survived but his original paint scheme has been uncovered including a frieze depicting scenes from Homer's *Iliad*. Now in the care of the NTS it is a unique opportunity to view a Thomson interior.

---

⑤ Turn right into **Belmont Street**, left at **Quad Gardens** then left again at **Queen Margaret Drive**. Cross the road and head down past the Botanic Gardens to turn right, back into **Great Western Road**. Cross the road and continue to **Great Western Terrace**, another Thomson masterpiece. Trace your steps back from here to the top of **Byres Road** and turn right then, near the bottom, turn left into **University Avenue**.

WHAT TO LOOK FOR ⓘ

As you exit the station into Gordon Street the first 'Greek' Thomson building is the former warehouse opposite. Look out for the **'Sixty Steps'** as you approach Queen Margaret Drive. There are remains of the former Queen Margaret Bridge on the left behind the BBC buildings. The 'Steps' used to lead from the bridge to Kelvinside Terrace West.

---

⑥ Turn left into **Oakfield Avenue**, pass **Eton Terrace** on the corner with Great George Street. Turn right into **Great George Street**, right at **Otago Street**, left into **Gibson Street** and keep going when it becomes **Eldon Street**. Finally turn right into **Woodlands Road** and return to Sauchiehall Street. Follow this to the junction with **Renfield Street**, turn right and head downhill to **Central Station**.

The Carbeth Hut Community

Discover a working class Utopian dream near the West Highland Way.

·DISTANCE·	3 miles (4.8km)
·MINIMUM TIME·	2hrs 30min
·ASCENT / GRADIENT·	98ft (30m) ▲ ▲ ▲
·LEVEL OF DIFFICULTY·	🚶 🚶 🚶
·PATHS·	Roads, access tracks and footpaths, 1 stile
·LANDSCAPE·	Hills, woodland and lochs
·SUGGESTED MAP·	aqua3 OS Explorer 348 Campsie Fells
·START / FINISH·	Grid reference: NX 524791
·DOG FRIENDLINESS·	Suitable for dogs
·PARKING·	Carbeth Inn, check beforehand with landlord
·PUBLIC TOILETS·	None on route

BACKGROUND TO THE WALK

Situated approximately half-way between Glasgow and Drymen on the A809, an old turnpike road, you'll find an ancient inn. At one time called the Halfway House and now the Carbeth Inn it has served the needs of travellers for well over 200 years. Sir Walter Scott had the character of Baillie Nicol Jarvie in his 1817 novel *Rob Roy* describe it as a 'most miserable alehouse'. Things have obviously improved since then and for years it has provided a warm welcome to climbers, bikers, walkers and the nearby community of Carbeth hutters.

Holidays in the Country
The Carbeth hut community started after World War One, when the owner of the Carbeth Estate let three ex-servicemen found a holiday fellowship camp on his land. At first the visitors lived under canvas but during the depression years unemployed Glaswegians, seeking an escape into the countryside, started to erect more permanent dwellings. These ingenious and often ramshackle affairs were constructed from any materials that were available free of charge or cheap. Conditions were spartan but met the needs of the people and were probably as good as they had at home. During the summers the area round the Carbeth Inn was alive with activity as whole families decamped to the countryside for their holidays.

Peppercorn Rent
The land was leased from estate owner, Barnes-Graham, at a peppercorn rent because of his desire to help people escape from what he saw as a squalid and depressing life in the crowded city. They became a tight-knit community with organised games and activities, they even built their own open-air swimming pool, complete with lifebelts and diving boards. To get to Carbeth the hutters took the train to Milngavie and then took to a path which became known as the Khyber Pass. Coming from the Clydebank area the hutters just hoofed it over the Kilpatrick Hills.

Scottish Social History

Today the swimming pool, simply a dammed stream, is silted up. Fashions and lifestyles have changed but Carbeth still has around 200 huts and an active community. However it is doubtful if it can be maintained for much longer. A massive increase in the rents led to a rent strike by many of the hutters and court action was initiated to evict them. Against a background of recriminations and accusations, not to mention unsolved arson attacks on huts belonging to members of their association, the Carbeth community are determined to preserve their unique foothold in the countryside. They are vigorously campaigning for public support and petitioning the Scottish Parliament in the hope that legislation can be passed to preserve this unique piece of Scottish social history and heritage.

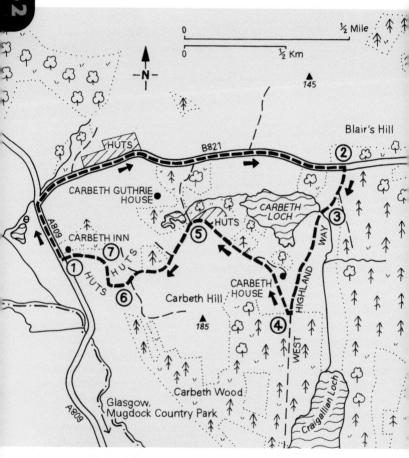

Walk 32 **Directions**

① From the car park at the **Carbeth Inn** turn right on to the **A809**. After ¼ mile (400m) take the first turning right on to the **B821**. Continue on this road for a mile

(1.6km) passing a collection of huts on the left and ignoring a public footpath sign to the right.

② Turn right at the signpost for the **West Highland Way**. There's also a Scottish Rights of Way Society signpost beside this pointing to the

Walk 32

WHILE YOU'RE THERE ⓘ
A visit to **Mugdock Country Park** is a great day out for families. A mere 3 miles (4.8km) from Carbeth it can be accessed by car or as an additional 6-mile (9.7km) round walking trip. In the visitor centre an audio visual theatre shows a selection of nature videos throughout the day at weekends. There are ranger-led activities, walking and orienteering trails and horse riding can be arranged at a local stable.

Khyber Pass Road to Mugdock Country Park. This was the favoured route of the early walkers heading out of Glasgow to the Campsie Fells and beyond.

③ Go through a gate and continue along a well-surfaced access road. Ignoring the Kyber Pass turn-off, keep right and go over a stile to follow the **West Highland Way** along the access road to more huts. After passing some huts on the right and another hut on the left look out for a partially concealed public path signpost on the right beside a West Highland Way marker post.

④ Turn right here on to a narrow but well-surfaced footpath and continue along it, passing **Carbeth Loch** on the right-hand side, to reach the junction with the drive leading to **Carbeth House**. This is a private house and is not open to the public. Turn left, pass a house on the right then take the next turning on the left.

⑤ Continue along this lane ignoring a public right of way sign pointing right, then head uphill to reach another grouping of the **Carbeth huts**. At the first hut, a green one, the road forks with a narrow path branching to the right. Ignore this and take the wider road which passes to the left of the hut.

⑥ Keep on this road as it passes through the main part of the **Carbeth huts**, an extraordinary assortment of small dwellings, shanties and shacks. Ignore all of the smaller tracks branching off this road. They allow access to individual huts or other parts of the settlement.

WHAT TO LOOK FOR ⓘ
If you have the time, and the inclination, look out for a road branching to the left after the first few huts in Point ⑤. Having an OS map will help here. This is the road that leads uphill, through a further group of huts, to give access to the top of **Carbeth Hill**. From this vantage point you will have a grand overview of the entire area and the extent of the hutters encampment.

⑦ Eventually pass a much larger hut on the right, then a smaller green one with a fenced garden on the left, and follow the road as it curves to the left. Continue downhill on this to reach the T-junction with the **A809** beside the **Carbeth Inn**. Turn right and return to the car park.

WHERE TO EAT AND DRINK ⓘ
Besides being the only option within any distance the **Carbeth Inn** is the finest hostelry in this part of Scotland. Retaining its old world ambience, it continues to offer an amazingly varied menu which contains everything from home-made soup, toasties and filled rolls to Scottish favourites like haggis, neeps and tatties and an all day breakfast which would keep a walker satisfied for many miles. Walkers are very welcome along with children and dogs.

Glasgow Harbour's Tall Ship

A pleasant walk by the last of the Clyde-built sailing ships.

•DISTANCE•	4¾ miles (7.7km)
•MINIMUM TIME•	3hrs 30min
•ASCENT / GRADIENT•	98ft (30m)
•LEVEL OF DIFFICULTY•	
•PATHS•	Pavements and footpaths
•LANDSCAPE•	Riverside, city blocks, park, botanic gardens
•SUGGESTED MAP•	aqua3 OS Explorer 342 Glasgow; AA Street by Street
•START / FINISH•	Grid reference: NS 569652
•DOG FRIENDLINESS•	Locals walk dogs on part of route, on lead on busy streets
•PARKING•	SECC car park beside Clyde Auditorium (Armadillo)
•PUBLIC TOILETS•	SECC

BACKGROUND TO THE WALK

When she was towed up the Clyde in 1993 the *Glenlee* was a sorry-looking sight. Little more than a derelict hulk, she had been saved from destruction by a group of forward-thinking enthusiasts. Today, restored to her former glory, she is an important part of the regeneration of Glasgow's harbour area.

From Cargo Vessel to Training Ship
Built in 1896 by Anderson Rodger & Co of Port Glasgow, the three-masted steel barque was one of the last sailing vessels launched on the Clyde. She had a long career as a cargo vessel, circumnavigating the globe four times and sailing over a million nautical miles under a British flag. Towards the end of her cargo career, engines were fitted to help keep her on schedule. Three times she ran aground and once almost caught fire, but on each occasion she was rescued. Then in 1921 she became a sail training ship for the Spanish Navy and remained in use until 1981. She sank at Seville, when her sea cocks were stolen to sell as scrap. With her engines drowned and rusted solid it looked like the end.

Lovingly Restored
The Clyde Maritime Trust received a letter from the Spanish Navy giving the ship's details and history and asking if the Trust would like to collect the *Glenlee* and save the ship from being broken up. The Trust had very little money but managed to raise enough to purchase, raise her and have her towed back to Scotland. After a short spell in dry dock at Greenock, where an inspection revealed the hull to be sound, the *Glenlee* was towed up the Clyde to Yorkhill Quay.

For the next six years volunteers and enthusiasts took on the seemingly impossible task of turning the *Glenlee* back into a sailing ship. The interior cargo holds and accommodation were lovingly re-created. Decking was fitted and Jamie White, a rigging expert from the National Maritime Museum in San Francisco, was called in to restore and reinstall the original rigging. White already looked after the rigging on the *Balclutha*, another Clyde-built sailing ship so he knew what he was doing. When work was nearly completed in 1999, the *Glenlee* was towed back down the Clyde to Greenock for the final paint job, known as

Gunport when dark patches were painted on the side to look like gun ports. In days gone by this 'deception' was thought to increase the safety of cargo ships. Old photographs of the *Glenlee* show that she was painted in Gunport at one time.

Fully restored, the *Glenlee* went on public display for the first time when the Tall Ships Race came to Greenock in 1999. Then it was a last tow up the Clyde to her permanent moorings at Yorkhill Quay.

Walk 33

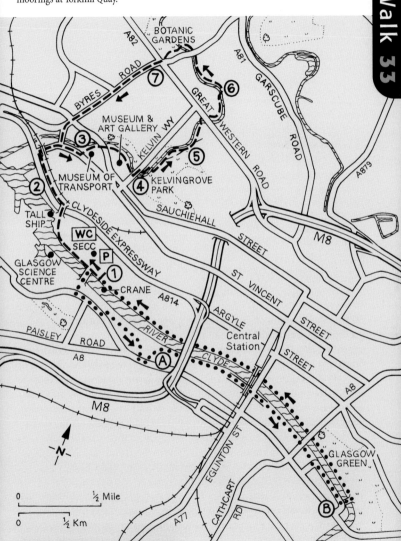

Walk 33 Directions

① From the **Scottish Exhibition and Conference Centre** (SECC) car park go on to the **Clyde Walkway**

and turn right, following signs to Pier 17, The Tall Ship and Museum of Transport (leave the route along here to visit the *Glenlee*). At the roundabout with the **Tall Ship** on the left, go over a pedestrian bridge to cross the **Clydeside Expressway**. Turn left and head west along the pavement beside a derelict building.

② Follow the footpath when it branches right and goes uphill, eventually coming to a junction. Go right under a railway bridge and continue on the pavement beside a high stone wall. Go right when you get to the next junction and along **Old Dumbarton Road** ignoring signs pointing both ways to the Kelvin Walkway. Cross the road, go over a bridge and turn left into **Bunhouse Road**.

WHERE TO EAT AND DRINK ⓘ

Take your pick from the **riverside café** passed on this walk, **coffee bars** within the SECC, the **restaurant** in the Italianate pumping house that forms the visitor centre for the Tall Ship, any one of a number of fine **restaurants** in Byres Road or the famous art deco **University Café** on the same street.

---

③ Pass the **Museum of Transport** on the right and, at the junction, cross the road via the pedestrian crossing and continue along a lane around **Kelvingrove Museum and Art Gallery**, through a car park and on to the T-junction with **Kelvin Way**. Turn left, go over a bridge and go right through a set of green gates on to the **Kelvin Walkway**.

④ The route is waymarked through **Kelvingrove Park**. Cross a bridge then pass the memorial to the Highland Light Infantry. Shortly after this there is a large bridge on the left and the path forks. Take the left path next to the river.

⑤ This eventually goes uphill. Just before the top of the hill look for a narrow path on the left through some bushes, which is easily missed.

Go left here and under a bridge. Turn left at the next waymark, go over a bridge and past a café/bar then continue along the walkway.

WHILE YOU'RE THERE ⓘ

Kelvingrove Museum and Art Gallery is an exciting place for the whole family to visit and needs at least half a day. Exhibits include period armour dating from medieval Europe to the body armour of a trooper from the *Star Wars* films, an extensive art collection and quirky exhibits like the Lakota Sioux Ghost Dance Shirt and the skeleton of a horse, once the subject of a court battle.

---

⑥ Cross another bridge, go left at a junction, still following the river. Go through a tunnel and then go left across a humpback bridge leading to the **Botanic Gardens**. Head up the steps to reach the gardens. When the path reaches a three-way junction take the second on the right. Pass the **Kibble Palace**, turn left and follow this drive to the gates and exit the gardens.

⑦ Cross **Great Western Road** at the traffic-lights and walk to the end of **Byres Road**. Cross **Dumbarton Road** and take the right fork. Take the second left, go along this street, cross a bridge and continue past a junction to the end of the street and under the railway bridge, turning left to return to the **SECC**.

WHAT TO LOOK FOR ⓘ

The massive glass **Kibble Palace** in the heart of the Botanic Gardens was not always here. Built at Coulport on Loch Long by the engineer John Kibble it was originally part of his own garden. In 1873 he gifted it to the Royal Botanic Institution who had it dismantled, shipped up the Clyde and rebuilt at its present site where it houses plants from the temperate zones.

The Clyde Walkway

Walk both sides of the Clyde from the Tall Ship to Glasgow Green.
See map and information panel for Walk 33

•DISTANCE•	5¾ miles (9.2km)
•MINIMUM TIME•	2hrs 30min
•ASCENT / GRADIENT•	Negligible
•LEVEL OF DIFFICULTY•	👫 👫 👫

Walk 34 Directions (Walk 33 option)

From the SECC car park cross the Clyde via **Bell's Bridge** towards the **Glasgow Science Centre**. At the end of the bridge keep straight ahead along the footpath. Look back to the Finnieston Crane – the largest crane in Europe when it was built in 1932 to hoist steam locomotives on board ships. At a T-junction with the main road, turn left. Follow this road to a roundabout and turn left. Go right along a quiet road through new housing. Turn left at the traffic-lights and then left along a pedestrian access to the Odeon cinema. Descend steps, cross a car park and turn right along the riverside walkway (Point Ⓐ).

At the end of the walkway turn right up steps then left along the street. At the next junction cross the road and go left. The road curves right to traffic-lights before a railway bridge. Go under the bridge and, at the next junction, cross at a pedestrian crossing into **Carleton Place**. At the end of this street continue along a footpath, up steps, cross the road and continue along the footpath. Go up some steps and turn left on to **Commercial Road**.

Keep following the river to a suspension bridge (Point Ⓑ). Cross to **Glasgow Green** and turn left.

This is Glasgow's main outdoor gathering place and was once the site of the Glasgow Fair. The large sandstone building at the centre is the People's Palace which covers Glasgow's social history. The ornate and colourful brick building near by is the former Templeton's Carpet Factory, modelled on the Doge's Palace in Venice.

At the end of Glasgow Green continue on the walkway along the banks of the **Clyde**. On your way back to the Armadillo you will pass a memorial to those who fought with the International Brigade during the Spanish Civil War. The little black statue of a woman with outstretched arms depicts Dolores Ibarruri, La Passionaria, a Spanish communist and freedom fighter, who famously declared, 'Better to die on your feet than live forever on your knees.'

A little further on is the *Waverley*, the last of the ocean-going paddle steamers. Now restored she still takes trippers 'doon the watter' each summer. Finally, just before the Armadillo and the SECC, is the **Finnieston Crane**.

The Antonine Wall and the Forth and Clyde Canal

Travel back in time along a Roman wall and an 18th-century canal.

•DISTANCE•	3½ miles (5.7km)
•MINIMUM TIME•	3hrs
•ASCENT / GRADIENT•	344ft (105m) ▲ ▲ ▲
•LEVEL OF DIFFICULTY•	🚶 🚶 🚶
•PATHS•	Canal tow path, farm road, footpath and road
•LANDSCAPE•	Canal, pastures, hillside and woodland
•SUGGESTED MAP•	aqua3 OS Explorer 348 Campsie Fells
•START / FINISH•	Grid reference: NS 719770
•DOG FRIENDLINESS•	Suitable for dogs, but keep on leads near livestock
•PARKING•	Car park near old quarry at Kilsyth
•PUBLIC TOILETS•	None on route

Walk 35 Directions

Exit the car park to the main road and turn right. Cross the road and take an immediate left on to a road, signed 'Twechar and Kirkintilloch'. Continue along this road for 200yds (183m). When the road turns sharply right, veer off the footpath to the left and on to the tow path of the **Forth and Clyde Canal**.

Before this canal was built ships had nearly 310 miles (499km) to sail round the coast of Scotland to get from west to east. When the canal was completed the journey was

reduced to 35 miles (56km). Construction began in 1768 with a team of navvies digging at Grangemouth on the Forth; 22 years later they finally reached Bowling on the Clyde.

This was the first canal built in Scotland and it was created for seagoing vessels. The 39 locks are all 60ft (18m) long and 20ft (6m) wide. It linked the two major waterways of the Clyde and the Forth. A further 3-mile (4.8km) branch was constructed from Maryhill to Port Dundas taking trade right to the heart of Glasgow.

Continue along the tow path until it rejoins the pavement beside the main road. Turn left, cross the canal via a bridge and enter **Twechar**.

The canal was purchased by the Caledonian Railway in 1868 and was the first canal to carry loaded railway wagons. In 1802 the trials of the *Charlotte Dundas*, Scotland's first steamboat, were conducted on

WHILE YOU'RE THERE ⓘ

The **Falkirk Wheel** is a miracle of modern engineering and the only rotating boat lift in the world. It can carry eight or more boats at a time on a trip taking a mere 15 minutes. When it opened in 2002 it reconnected the Forth and Clyde and Union canals making it once more possible to travel from the west to the east coast, overland, by boat.

the canal and Scotland's first iron boat, *The Vulcan*, was built for a passenger service on the canal in 1818. The canal continued to operate into the 20th century and finally closed to navigation in 1963. Now after extensive restoration and the creation of the revolutionary Falkirk Wheel (➤ While You're There) it is once more open throughout its entire length.

Continue on this road, heading uphill to a sign on the left pointing to the Antonine Wall and Bar Hill. Turn left on to this access road. Continue along here past some houses and continue on a farm track. Go through a gate and uphill. Look back the way you have come for a grand view of the canal as it winds its way towards Glasgow.

The canal followed the line of the Roman Antonine Wall. This frontier defence was begun by the governor of Britain, Lollius Urbicus, in AD 142, at the time of the Emperor Antoninus Pius. Like the more famous Hadrian's Wall further south, it was intended to keep the warlike Pictish tribes of the north out of Roman territory. But Lowland Scotland had not been completely subdued and, on more than one occasion, the remnants of hostile tribes forced the Romans back to the safety of Hadrian's Wall. The Romans finally gave up and left Scotland about AD 180.

When you reach the entrance to the **Antonine Wall** go left through a kissing gate and along a grassy lane then through another kissing gate to access the site. Veer left and uphill to **Bar Hill Fort**. A series of forts, fortlets and beacon platforms were spaced along the 37-mile (60km) length of the wall. This one is about 200ft (61m) south of the wall and as you explore the site you can see traces of the west, north and east ramparts and ditches. Look also for the foundations and outline of the bathhouse and latrines.

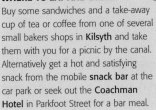

From the top of the fort you will see some woodland in front of you. Head for an opening in the trees and go on to a well-defined trail. Follow this through the trees and up on to the summit of **Castle Hill**. From here head downhill with the remains of the Antonine Wall on your left. The foundations were made of stone and on them was set a rampart of turf with a ditch in front. The Military Way, a Roman road for moving troops ran to the south of the road from the Clyde to the Forth. Turn right when your path is blocked by a dry-stone wall and follow it until you intersect a farm track. Turn left and follow this, crossing a gate, to a T-junction with the main road. Turn left and head downhill. Keep left at the roundabout and at the T-junction cross the road to return to the car park.

Exploring the Whangie

Through the hidden opening to the training ground of generations of rock climbers.

•DISTANCE•	2½ miles (4km)
•MINIMUM TIME•	3hrs
•ASCENT / GRADIENT•	515ft (157m) ▲▲▲
•LEVEL OF DIFFICULTY•	🚶🚶 🚶🚶 🚶🚶
•PATHS•	Hill tracks and well-trodden footpaths, 2 stiles
•LANDSCAPE•	Hill, woodland and lochs
•SUGGESTED MAP•	aqua3 OS Explorer 347 Loch Lomond South
•START / FINISH•	Grid reference: NS 511808
•DOG FRIENDLINESS•	Suitable for dogs, but keep on lead near livestock
•PARKING•	Queen's View car park
•PUBLIC TOILETS•	None on route

BACKGROUND TO THE WALK

Queen Victoria stood near the start of this walk for her first view of Loch Lomond. She never ventured further up the hill and so missed the opportunity to explore the Whangie, a strange cleft in the rock that has fascinated generations of rock climbers.

A Gash in the Rock

Geologists would have us believe that this gash in the rocks, 50ft (15m) deep and 300ft (91m) long, was caused by a landslide, when the surface layer of black basalt moved slowly over the underlying sandstone. This created stresses within the basalt, which eventually fractured, producing thin slices of slab. However, ask any local about the Whangie and you will be told the truth. It was created by the Devil himself on his way to a witches' coven near Stockie Muir. He got so excited that he gave one flick of his mighty tail and carved a slice out of the hillside creating the Whangie. Whang is a common Lowland Scots dialect word meaning a slice.

Early Pioneers

Whatever its origin, the Whangie is still a valued training ground for Glasgow rock climbers, successors to the mountaineering pioneers of the 1920s and 30s. These working class men from Glasgow started walking out of the city to explore the surrounding countryside. Clad only in their ordinary clothes and with little in the way of equipment, save perhaps some army surplus kit or an old clothes line, they went looking for adventure.

After a hard week of work they would leave Glasgow late at night, take the last bus to the outskirts and walk into the countryside. They had no tents and found shelter where they could, under a hedge, behind a dry-stone wall or in a cave. Some of the great names in Scottish climbing were amongst these early pioneers, including W H Murray, the celebrated Himalayan climber and environmentalist, and Tom Weir, who climbed with Murray and went on to make a series of television programmes called *Weir's Way*. Weir continued to write a monthly column of his outdoor adventures in the *Scots Magazine* until he was in his late eighties.

Escaping the Slums

From Glasgow they would head to Milngavie and a campfire near Craigallion Loch. Some, like the legendary Jock Nimlin, were fortunate to have friends who possessed huts at Carbeth (▶ Walk 32), not far from Craigallion and from there they would walk out, 'up the pipe', to Loch Katrine in the Trossachs. They explored all the glorious countryside they could see from the hills around the Whangie – Ben Lomond, the Kilpatrick Hills and the Arrochar Alps. During prolonged periods of unemployment in the depression years these hardy climbers and others like them took to the hills every week to escape the slums of Glasgow. Some even walked all the way to the Highlands.

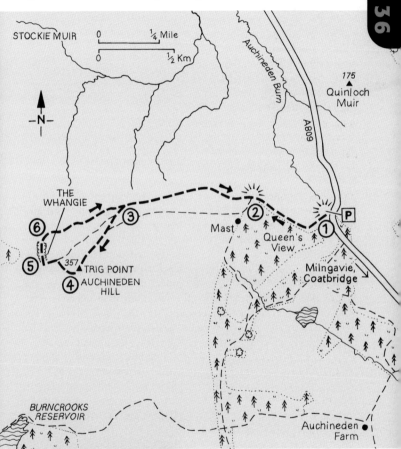

Walk 36 Directions

① Head toward the left of the car park on to the small hillock where Queen Victoria stood for her first breathtaking view of Loch Lomond. Descend and cross a stile over the wall where a well-defined path crosses duckboards and meanders uphill. Turn right to follow the edge of a wood. After the duckboards this is a pleasant grassy walk.

② As you get to the top, near a fence, stop for a while to admire the view. Look away to your right for the expanse of Loch Lomond, Ben

Walk 36

Lomond towering over it to the right and the Arrochar Hills away to the left. Cross a ladder stile over the fence and turn right on to a narrow but well-trodden path. Follow this along the side of the hill.

③ When the path forks go left and head uphill. As you near the top you will see the Ordnance Survey pillar on the summit of **Auchineden Hill**. Head towards this by any route you can find. The ground round here is often boggy and several attempts may be required to find the best way across it. To the south from here are the Kilpatrick Hills and, beyond them, the River Clyde. Look for **Burncrooks Reservoir** to your right and **Kilmannan Reservoir** to your left. Beyond that is Cochno Loch, another reservoir and a favourite excursion for the residents of nearby Clydebank.

> **WHILE YOU'RE THERE** ⓘ
> **Summerlee Heritage Park** is based in an old ironworks at Coatbridge east of Glasgow. The history of steel and heavy engineering is what's on offer here in Scotland's noisiest museum. Local engineers demonstrate daily the workings of the historic machines and are busy making spares to restore others. There's a reconstructed tinsmith's shop, brass foundry and spade shop plus rides on an old tramcar along some re-laid track.

> **WHERE TO EAT AND DRINK** ⓘ
> The superb **Carbeth Inn** (► Walk 32) is the nearest eating place just over a mile (1.6km) south of the car park on the A809. Here you will find a warm welcome for walkers, a wonderful ambience, real ales and everything from an all day breakfast to home-made soup, sandwiches, snacks and main meals.

④ Looking towards Ben Lomond, the area in front of you is the Stockie Muir, where the Devil was heading for the tryst that created the Whangie. Walk towards the Ben on a path leading away from the Ordnance Survey pillar and go downhill into a dip. Another path runs across this. Turn left on to it and follow it round the side of a small hill. Where the path curves right look for crags on the right.

⑤ This is where you'll find the hidden opening to **the Whangie**. It's easy to miss so look out for a spot on the right where it is easy. Climb a few steps up to the crags and it's as if the wall opens up in front of you. Climb into the Whangie and walk to the other end on a path.

⑥ Exit the Whangie and head to the right on another footpath. Continue on this until it rejoins the path you took on the uphill journey. Go back to the stile then retrace your steps downhill and back to the car park.

> **WHAT TO LOOK FOR** ⓘ
> A variety of wild plants and flowers can be found on this walk. Look for several varieties of fern on the way. At the Whangie look for **wood sorrel** with its shamrock shaped leaves and white flowers with five petals and lilac veins. At the entrance to the chasm are more ferns, heather and red campion, an early summer flower whose blooms open by day to attract butterflies and bees.

First climbed, with Benny & Ramy, on perfect morning of 22/5/04, with picnic @ Whangie.

Through the Queen Elizabeth Forest Park

Walking across the Highland Boundary Fault and along a 19th-century inclined railway.

•DISTANCE•	4 miles (6.4km)
•MINIMUM TIME•	3hrs
•ASCENT / GRADIENT•	446ft (136m) ▲▲▲
•LEVEL OF DIFFICULTY•	🚶🚶 🚶🚶 🚶🚶
•PATHS•	Forest roads and footpaths
•LANDSCAPE•	Forest and hills
•SUGGESTED MAP•	aqua3 OS Explorer 365 The Trossachs
•START / FINISH•	Grid reference: NN 519014
•DOG FRIENDLINESS•	Suitable for well-behaved dogs
•PARKING•	At visitor centre near Aberfoyle
•PUBLIC TOILETS•	At visitor centre

BACKGROUND TO THE WALK

This walk crosses the Highland Boundary Fault, a geological line stretching across the country from Arran to Stonehaven just south of Aberdeen. It is one of Britain's most important geological features and it separates the Highlands from the Lowlands. This weak line in the crust of the earth formed around 390 million years ago when the old rocks of the Highlands were forced up and the Lowland rocks pushed down.

North of the fault lie Highland rocks, created over 500 million years ago when land movement on a massive scale squeezed and heated the stone. Whinstone, which was used extensively as a building stone because it splits easily, formed from extreme pressure on mud and sand. Slate was also formed in this fashion but was compressed into layers and was valued as a roofing material.

Slate Quarry

Near the walk is the Duke's Pass, one of the largest slate quarries in Scotland. Most of the higher mountains are formed from a rock known as Leny Gritt, which started life as sand and gravel before being moulded into shape by intense heat and pressure. Another group of rocks includes Achray Sandstone, formed when this high mountain area was under the sea. Later earth movement caused the sandstone to tip and stand on its end. Iron minerals present in the formation of the sandstone gave it a reddish brown colour.

Inclined Railway

Given the quality and variety of the rocks found in this part of the forest park it is unsurprising that in the past a great deal of quarrying took place here. Evidence of a once thriving quarry can be found on the steep downhill path (Point ④ in the Directions), which, at the beginning of the 19th century, was an inclined railway transporting the limestone from Lime Craig Quarry. The limestone was carried on wooden wagons to the lime kilns which used to be at the bottom of the hill.

Heavy wooden sleepers supported the three rails of the wagon way. Full wagons went down using the centre and one outside rail while the empties returned on the centre and other outside rail. The wagons were attached to a wire rope, which was wound round a drum at the top of the hill enabling the weight of the full wagons and gravity to provide the power to return the empty ones to the top. Half way up the track was a short section of double railing to allow the wagons to pass each other. Brakes at the top of the incline could be used to control the rate of descent. By 1850 the quarry was worked out and the wagon way no longer needed.

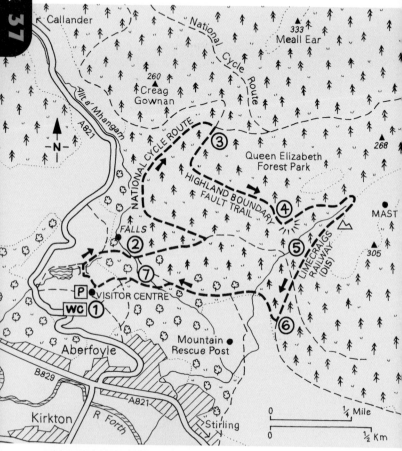

Walk 37 **Directions**

① From the front of the visitor centre turn left, go down some steps on to a well-surfaced footpath and follow the blue waymarkers of the **Highland Boundary Fault Trail**. Continue on this trail to reach the **Waterfall of the Little Fawn** with

its 55ft (16.7m) drop. Shortly after this turn left to cross a bridge then turn right following the white arrow left again on to a forest road.

② This is part of the National Cycle Network (NCN) so look out for cyclists. Head uphill on this waymarked road following the blue Highland Boundary Fault markers and the NCN Route 7 signs. When the road forks at a junction, keep left continuing uphill until you reach a crossroads.

③ Turn right, at the blue waymarker, on to a smaller and rougher road. The Boundary Fault Trail parts company with the NCN Route 7 at this point. The going is easy along this fairly level section. Keep going until you eventually reach a viewpoint on the right with a strategically placed seat.

④ From here the road heads uphill until it reaches a waymarker near a path heading uphill towards a mast. Turn right then go through a barrier and start descending. Although this is a well-made path it is nevertheless a very steep descent through the woods and great care should be taken.

WHILE YOU'RE THERE
Blair Drummond Safari Park, on the road between Doune and Stirling, is a credible day out for the whole family and the only wildlife park in Scotland. Here you'll see animals ranging from lions and elephants, camels and bison roaming free. Other attractions include a pet farm, pedal boats and a waterfowl cruise.

⑤ This path follows the line of the Limecraigs Railway an early 19th-century inclined railway used for transporting limestone. It continues downhill to go through another barrier where the path is intersected by a forest road. Cross this road, go through another barrier and once again head downhill.

⑥ At the bottom of the hill is a set of steps leading to a forest road. Turn right on to the road and follow the blue waymarkers. Stay on this road until you reach a green

WHERE TO EAT AND DRINK
The **visitor centre** at the Queen Elizabeth Forest Park contains an excellent restaurant where you can enjoy a bowl of hot soup, various hot and cold drinks and a host of other delights ranging from sandwiches to hot meals. As an accompaniment to the food you can enjoy some spectacular views over the forest park.

signpost on the left pointing to the visitor centre. Turn left on to a downhill track and head through the woods.

⑦ Eventually you will reach a board announcing the end of the trail. From here the route is signed back to the **visitor centre**. When the trail forks take the right-hand turning and head uphill beside a handrail and return to the start.

WHAT TO LOOK FOR
The surrounding **forest** is made up of species such Sitka spruce, Douglas fir, oak, Scots pine, larch, birch and Norway spruce. In January 1968 a gale destroyed large areas of the woodland and the opportunity was taken to clear and replant. Around these areas are more mature plantings from the 1930s and later ones from the 1980s.

The Great Forest of Loch Ard

One of Scotland's great woodlands, hiding place of the Stone of Destiny and birthplace of the Scottish Parliament.

•DISTANCE•	3½ miles (5.7km)
•MINIMUM TIME•	2hrs
•ASCENT / GRADIENT•	98ft (30m) ▲ ▲ ▲
•LEVEL OF DIFFICULTY•	󰀀 󰀀 󰀀
•PATHS•	Roads, forest roads and trails
•LANDSCAPE•	Fields, hills, forest and loch
•SUGGESTED MAP•	aqua3 OS Explorer 365 The Trossachs
•START / FINISH•	Grid reference: NS 521009
•DOG FRIENDLINESS•	Keep under control or on lead to avoid disturbing wildlife
•PARKING•	Car park at Aberfoyle beside tourist office in centre of town
•PUBLIC TOILETS•	Beside tourist office next to car park

BACKGROUND TO THE WALK

Lying between the town of Aberfoyle and the foothills of Ben Lomond this huge area of woodland is part of the Queen Elizabeth Forest Park. It stretches from just north of Drymen almost to the banks of Loch Katrine. It may look like just another conifer plantation but a walk through any part of it will reveal a surprising variety of landscapes, flora and fauna.

Forestry Management

Most of the forested land was purchased by the Forestry Commission in the early 1930s. It was planted straight away and by the closing years of the century consisted of mature woodland. Ongoing thinning started in the 1950s and areas were felled towards the end of the century. Some 60,000 tons of timber are extracted each year from the park as a whole. With the United Kingdom currently importing about 90 per cent of its timber needs, the increase in harvesting the park's mature trees will help to reduce this figure.

The area south of Lochan Spling was initially planted with Norway spruce, Sitka spruce, larch and Scots pine. Most of the spruce together with some of the larch and pine was felled in the 1980s and replaced with Douglas fir, larch and Sitka spruce. But native broadleaves have been planted too, including 10,000 oak trees to augment the remains of the ancient oak woods that once covered most of the area. Birch and rowan have been regenerating naturally. Part of this area has been left to mature to provide magnificent specimens the equal of anything in European forests. The entire area is enclosed within a deer fence to let the trees have a chance to establish.

Wilderness Areas

Wildlife is abundant, including red squirrels and capercaillie. Decaying pines, which have been uprooted in gales or just collapsed, support wood boring insects and provide a ready food supply for a whole host of birds. There are peat bogs and wilderness areas like the one just south of Duchray water in the old wood of Drumore. Here there are no trails, but amidst this jungle-like habitat can be found blueberry, chickweed, wintergreen, cow-wheat and cowberry. You will probably see some evidence of red and roe deer and if you are really quiet may see rare birds like blackcock and woodpecker.

Changing attitudes to conservation and forestry management have helped to bring about a gradual reshaping of the forest to provide a more diverse range of tree species, a wider range of habitats and an environment rich in wildlife.

Stop at the Covenanters Inn where the Nationalists, led by John McCormick, met in 1949 to launch a petition, which they called the Second Covenant. The signatories called on the government of the day to give Scotland a devolved parliament. Over 2 million people signed the petition but it was not until the closing years of the 20th century, and after much argument, campaigning and voting, that their wishes were granted.

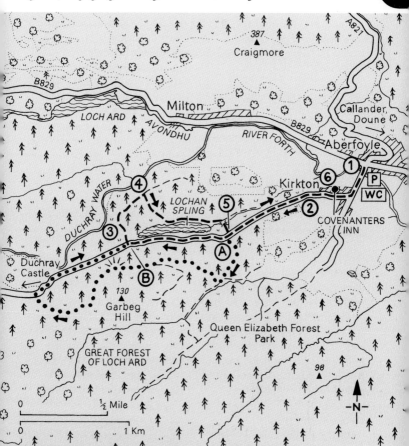

Walk 38 Directions

① Leave from the west end of the car park and turn left into **Manse Road**. Cross a narrow bridge over

the **River Forth** (the river has its source near here although it is more usually associated with Edinburgh) and continue along the grass beside the road until the first junction on the right. Turn right here and head

Walk 38

uphill, passing the **Covenanters Inn**. A short distance past here is open countryside and the start of the Great Forest of Loch Ard.

② Head straight on along the forest road, keeping an ear open for heavy timber lorries. During the week this can get fairly busy, as this is a main forestry extraction route, so keep well into the side. After approximately ½ mile (800m) you will reach a staggered crossroads. Continue straight ahead along the forest road until you come to a turning on the right with a yellow waymarker. Turn right here.

> **WHERE TO EAT AND DRINK** ℹ
> The excellent **Forth Inn** is reached from the car park. In good weather meals and refreshments are served on picnic tables at the front of the inn or within the spacious, non-smoking, restaurant. Delicious home-made soups are served with fresh crusty bread or choices can be made from the full menu and specials board. They also have toys and colouring books to keep children amused.

③ Follow this waymarked trail through the forest almost to the banks of **Duchray Water**. This rises on the north face of Ben Lomond and joins with the Avondhu from Loch Ard to create the River Forth near Aberfoyle. The path curves right, continues to descend slightly and then reaches a junction.

> **WHAT TO LOOK FOR** ℹ
> The Trossachs is an area rich in wildlife. **Roe deer** is the animal you have the best chance of seeing on the walk. However with a bit of luck, and by keeping quiet, you could also happen on to some of the rarer beasties which inhabit these woods and hills. This is the southern limit for the elusive **pine marten** and some have been spotted round Loch Ard.

④ Turn right and follow the path through the trees to the north banks of **Lochan Spling**. The path then swings left and, at the end of the Lochan, turns right at a waymarker pole, crosses a small stream and heads slightly uphill.

⑤ When the path reaches the T-junction, turn left and rejoin the main forest access road continuing along it to the **Covenanters Inn**. This takes its name not from the activities of the 17th-century Scottish Presbyterians, who were persecuted by the Stuart monarchy for refusing to give up their faith, but to the activities of 20th-century Scottish Nationalists.

⑥ Continue past the inn, where a later group of Nationalists temporarily hid Scotland's Stone of Destiny when it was liberated from Westminster Abbey in 1950, then turn left on to **Manse Road** at the junction and return to the start.

> **WHILE YOU'RE THERE** ℹ
> Pay a visit to **Doune Castle**, 13 miles (20.9km) east of Aberfoyle, built in the 14th century for the Duke of Albany. It was a ruin by the 18th century but has since been restored and now offers a look at what life was like in a medieval royal household. It featured in the film *Monty Python and the Holy Grail* (1974) and more recently the BBC dramatisation of *Ivanhoe*.
> Although usually associated with the City of Edinburgh, the **River Forth** actually rises near here where the Duchray Water meets the Avondhu River. It increases in size by the addition of the River Teith near Stirling then continues its journey to the coast and flows under the famous Forth Bridges at Queensferry.

And on to the Duchray Estate

Mustering point for Royalist troops and a bolt hole for Rob Roy MacGregor.
See map and information panel for Walk 38

•DISTANCE•	6 miles (9.7km)
•MINIMUM TIME•	3hrs 30min
•ASCENT / GRADIENT•	164ft (50m) ▲ ▲ ▲
•LEVEL OF DIFFICULTY•	👫 👫 👫

Walk 39 Directions
(Walk 38 option)

At the staggered crossroads (Point Ⓐ), leave the main track and turn left on to a narrower one marked by a blue Forest Enterprise waymarker pole. From here head uphill, go through a gate and continue up the hill. At a fork in the path take the right-hand turn. Then, ignoring a turning to the right beside another waymarker post, keep straight ahead.

The path continues, still climbing steeply uphill, to reach a viewpoint on the right-hand side near the top of the hill. Stop for a minute here and enjoy the panoramic views across to Loch Ard and the forest to the slopes of Ben Venue. A short distance further on there is another viewpoint on the right.

This is part of Duchray Estate, which also gives its name to Duchray Castle a 16th-century keep built by the Grahams of Downie. This was the mustering point for an army raised in 1653 by William, 9th Earl of Glencairn to fight for restoration of the Stuart monarchy.

He led 4,000 men in open battle against Cromwell's army and won a minor victory, near Aberfoyle, against government forces under the command of Captain Kidd of Stirling Castle. The insurrection was, however, short lived and was put down by General Monk, who then burned the castle at Duchray. It was rebuilt and is now in private hands and not open to the public.

During another turbulent period in Scotland's past Duchray provided shelter, on at least one occasion, to Rob Roy MacGregor (1672–1734). This folk hero or bandit, depending on your point of view (► Walk 42), roamed and raided extensively in this area, seizing cattle and capturing rent money. Not surprisingly he was often pursued by the forces of law and order.

From the viewpoint the path starts its journey downhill again and eventually terminates at a T-junction by two stone cottages. Turn right, back on to the wider forest access road, and continue along it until you reach a yellow waymarker, at a turning on the left, on to a narrower path. Turn left to rejoin the main walk at Point Ⓑ around **Lochan Spling**.

Up the Doon Hill

A circular walk in the footsteps of Robert Kirk, the minister who believed in fairies.

•DISTANCE•	2 miles (3.2km)
•MINIMUM TIME•	2hrs 30min
•ASCENT / GRADIENT•	220ft (67m) ▲▲▲
•LEVEL OF DIFFICULTY•	🚶 🚶 🚶
•PATHS•	Roads, forest roads and well-surfaced footpaths
•LANDSCAPE•	Pastures, hills and woods
•SUGGESTED MAP•	aqua3 OS Explorer 365 The Trossachs
•START / FINISH•	Grid reference: NS 521009
•DOG FRIENDLINESS•	Suitable for dogs
•PARKING•	Car park in Aberfoyle next to tourist office
•PUBLIC TOILETS•	Beside tourist office next to car park

Walk 40 Directions

From the west end of the car park exit on to **Manse Road** and turn left. Immediately cross a narrow bridge over the **River Forth** and continue along the road to the cemetery. Enter through a pair of ornate metal gates and cross over to the remains of the church.

Standing on either side of the doorway into the church are two heavy iron objects shaped like coffins. These are mort safes and if you try to lift them you will find them almost impossible to move. They were placed over the coffins of the newly deceased and kept there until the bodies were judged as being decomposed. This was for fear of raids by grave robbers. It was at a time when medical science was advancing and anatomists in the great medical schools of Edinburgh and Glasgow needed a constant supply of fresh cadavers. They were prepared to pay handsomely with no questions asked. The grave

robbers were called Burkers after the notorious Burke and Hare, the Edinburgh grave robbers and murderers of the early 19th century.

Walk from here to the rear of the church and look for a carving with what looks like a dagger crossed with a hook. This marks the burial place of one of Kirkton's ministers, the Revd Robert Kirk. But as any local will tell you, the minister is elsewhere, as you will discover.

From here return to the main gate, leave the churchyard and turn left to continue along **Manse Road**. Go past some houses and pick up the signs pointing to Fairy Hill. Continue along the forest road and don't be surprised if you come across people with teams of huskies

---

WHERE TO EAT AND DRINK ⓘ
The **Forth Inn** near the car park, offers a full menu and specials in the restaurant.. Delicious home-made soups are served with fresh crusty bread. In good weather you can enjoy your meal outside at the picnic tables.

and sleds in winter. As you continue through a gate you will see a sign explaining that this is a Husky Training Route. Near the top of the hill there's a sign pointing to the left and the **Doon Hill Fairy Trail Circular Walk**.

By modern standards the Revd Kirk would be regarded as barking mad but in the 17th century a belief in fairies was not considered strange, even in the local minister. It was the Revd Kirk's daily practice to walk to the top of Doon Hill, known as the fairy knoll and, according to tradition, the home of fairies. The Revd Kirk, himself, was the seventh son of the minister of Aberfoyle, something in itself believed to endow a person with magical powers like the second sight.

WHAT TO LOOK FOR ℹ️

Look out on Manse Road for a large **oak tree**, called the poker tree. This refers to a story in Scott's *Rob Roy* where Baillie Nicol Jarvie enters an Aberfoyle inn in defiance of warning to keep out. A fight ensues with the inhabitants and the Baillie, finding his sword rusted in the scabbard, grabs a red hot poker from the fire and uses it, setting a Highlander on fire.

Follow the steps of the minister by turning left on to a well-surfaced gravel footpath. Follow it uphill, through the trees and up several sets of steps. Eventually reach the summit of the hill, which is covered in trees.

It was here that the Revd Kirk studied the fairy people and found out all about their habits, homes, superstitions, work and food. He talked to anyone who claimed to have met the fairies. When he had collected enough information he

wrote a book about them called *The Secret Commonwealth of Elves, Fauns and Fairies*. It was written in 1691, eventually published in 1815 and is still being studied by folklorists today.

Legend has it that this telling of tales incurred the wrath of the fairy folk, who were displeased by the fact that mortals could now find out all about them. They spirited the minister away and imprisoned him for eternity on Doon Hill. In reality he died of a heart attack in 1692, on the summit of the hill. He was buried in his own churchyard but again tradition has it that the fairies substituted a changeling for the burial and that the Revd Kirk is imprisoned in a tree on the hill.

As you walk around the top of the hill, you will see coloured cloths, scarves, hats and other objects on the branches of the trees. These are offerings to the fairies from visitors. Some messages are attached, mostly asking the fairies to help them.

Returning from the summit, take the opposite path from the one you came up. But look back as you leave at the tallest and most prominent tree on the hill. That's where the Revd Kirk is supposed to be incarcerated. Leave the hill and follow the path downhill to rejoin the forest road and turn right. Retrace your steps back to the car park.

WHILE YOU'RE THERE ℹ️

Take the ferry from Port of Menteith and visit **Inchmahome**, the largest of three islands on Lake of Mentieth. It contains the ruins of the 13th-century priory used by Mary, Queen of Scots to hide from the English in 1547. A walk around the island take about half an hour.

Walk 41

A Trail Through the Sallochy Woods

A gentle stroll by the bonnie banks of Loch Lomond.

•DISTANCE•	2 miles (3.2km)
•MINIMUM TIME•	2hrs 30min
•ASCENT / GRADIENT•	131ft (40m)
•LEVEL OF DIFFICULTY•	
•PATHS•	West Highland Way, forest trail and forest road
•LANDSCAPE•	Loch, hills and woodland
•SUGGESTED MAP•	aqua3 OS Explorer 364 Loch Lomond North
•START / FINISH•	Grid reference: NS 380957
•DOG FRIENDLINESS•	Suitable for dogs
•PARKING•	Sallochy Woods car park
•PUBLIC TOILETS•	None on route

BACKGROUND TO THE WALK

One of Scotland's best-known songs, *The Bonnie Banks of Loch Lomond*, was reputedly written by a soldier of Prince Charles Edward Stuart's army during the Jacobite rising of 1745. During the long, slow retreat from Derby the soldier was captured and taken to Carlisle Castle and it was here that he wrote the song for his love, while languishing in prison awaiting execution. It tells of their joy in each other's company on the banks of Loch Lomond and how she would make the lonely journey home to Scotland by the 'high road'. Meanwhile his soul would be instantly transported at the moment of death back to his beloved loch along the 'low road' of the underworld and reach there before her. It's a poignant song of love and parting and a nostalgic remembrance of a landscape that the soldier will never see again in life.

Loch Lomond

Loch Lomond is the largest fresh water lake in Britain. It is 24 miles (38.6km) long, 5 miles (8km) wide and, at its deepest point is 623ft (190m) deep. Within its banks are approximately 38 islands, some of which are inhabited while others form sanctuaries for birds and wildlife. Most of them are in private ownership and not open to visitors. Inchcailloch is part of the National Nature Reserve and Bucinch and Ceardach are National Trust for Scotland properties. They can be visited and in summer a ferry and mail boat operate a regular passenger service from the boatyard at Balmaha, allowing island exploration and the opportunity to lunch at the Inchmurrin Hotel on Inchmurrin.

Geological Fault

The loch straddles the Highland Boundary Fault, a fracture caused by movement of the earth's crust millions of years ago, and the geological differences between Highland and Lowland Scotland are clearly visible from its banks. Here the fault runs from Conic Hill on the south east shore and through the islands of Inchcailloch, Torrinch, Creinch and Inchmurrin.

Forest Park

Most visitors rush up the busy A82 along the west side of Loch Lomond, but on the more secluded eastern shore there is a largely unspoilt area of tranquillity and beauty, even in the height of summer. The diverse woods here are part of the Queen Elizabeth Forest Park and contain walking and nature trails and isolated picnic spots. The variety of animals and plants which can be found is staggering. Over a quarter of the plants that flourish in Britain can be found around the loch. You may well spot the rare capercaillie (it's the size of a turkey), ptarmigan or even a golden eagle. On Inchcailloch white fallow deer have been spotted in the past. While on Inchconnacan you might encounter a wallaby. They were transported here from the Australian outback some years ago, by Lady Arran.

Walk 41 Directions

① From the car park head towards the entrance on to the main road. Go right on to a track beside the starting post to the **Sallochy Trail**. Cross the road with care and continue along the trail on the other side. This runs alongside some woodland which you should keep on your your right-hand side. Continue and, when the path eventually forks, keep right and go into the wood following the obvious waymarker posts.

② The trail goes through the wood and passes into the ruined 19th-century farm steading of **Wester Sallochy** which the Forestry Commission has now cleared of trees. Several buildings can be seen and its worth spending some time investigating these old ruins and trying to imagine life in those times. When you have finished, circle the buildings to the left and follow the well-worn trail until it ends at a T-junction beside a waymarker post. Turn right on to the forest road here.

③ Follow the forest road for about ½ mile (800m) to reach a gate just

before the junction with the main road. Cross the gate, then cross the main road and turn right. Look carefully for a faint track running through the woods to your left.

④ Follow the faint track back towards the loch (if you miss the track then enter the wood at any point and head west towards the loch). When the track intersects with a well-surfaced footpath turn right. You are now on the **West Highland Way**. Follow the waymarkers, keeping on the main path and ignoring any subsidiary tracks branching off it.

⑤ Follow the path uphill through a rocky section and then, as it levels off, through a wood. There is some boggy ground here but strategically placed duckboards make the going easier. Eventually the trail passes through the **Sallochy Woods** car park returning you to the start.

From Balquhidder to Creag an Tuirc

*On the trail of the Highland outlaw, Rob Roy, a 'MacGregor despite them',
and on to his final resting place.*

•DISTANCE•	2½ miles (4km)
•MINIMUM TIME•	2hrs
•ASCENT / GRADIENT•	328ft (100m) ▲▲▲
•LEVEL OF DIFFICULTY•	🚶 🚶 🚶
•PATHS•	Forest roads and hillside, 2 stiles
•LANDSCAPE•	Hills, loch and woodlands
•SUGGESTED MAP•	aqua3 OS Explorer 365 The Trossachs
•START / FINISH•	Grid reference: NN 536209
•DOG FRIENDLINESS•	Dogs ok on this route
•PARKING•	At Balquhidder church
•PUBLIC TOILETS•	None on route

BACKGROUND TO THE WALK

Immortalised in the 19th century by Sir Walter Scott in his novel *Rob Roy* (1817), the
romantic myth of Rob Roy MacGregor's life has more recently been retold in the 1995 film
of the same name starring Liam Neeson and Jessica Lange.

Prosperous Cattle Dealer

Born in 1671, the third son of Lieutenant Colonel Donald MacGregor of Glengyle, Rob Roy
was exceedingly strong, with long arms. Roy, from the Gaelic rhuadh, meaning red, denoted
the colour of his hair. After his marriage to Mary Campbell he acquired land on the east
shore of Loch Lomond and rented grazing at Balquhidder. Soon he was a prosperous cattle
dealer but an arrangement with the Marquis of Montrose led to his downfall. In 1711 the
Marquis gave Rob Roy £1,000 to buy cattle, one of his men absconded with the money and
Rob Roy was charged with embezzlement. Failure to answer the court summons led to him
being outlawed and a warrant issued for his arrest. Meanwhile Montrose's factor, Graham of
Killearn, evicted Rob Roy's wife and family from their home at Craigroyston.

To Outlaw

The Earl of Breadalbane gave Rob Roy some land in Glen Dochart, but as an outlaw he was
unable to trade as a cattle dealer. Undeterred he turned to sheep and cattle rustling and
offering protection. He harried far and wide, lifting cattle and demanding blackmail. His
most vicious attacks were always reserved for the Marquis of Montrose, stealing his cattle
and lifting his rents. He was even known to give money to a tenant facing eviction and then
ambush the factor to steal it back.

Twice Rob Roy was captured but both times he managed to escape. Once in a daring
escapade, while fording the River Forth and tied to a horse behind his captors, he severed
his bonds and plunged into the fast flowing river. His captors were powerless as the current
swept him down river.

In 1715 he raised Clan Gregor for the Jacobite rising of the Old Pretender. When it failed, Rob Roy was charged with high treason but again he managed to give his pursuers the slip and retain his freedom. Government forces burnt his house in Glen Dochart, but in 1716 the Duke of Argyll let him build another in Glen Shira.

Pardoned

After years of being a wanted man he finally turned himself in to General Wade in 1725 and was pardoned by the King. His remaining years were spent in his house at Inverlochlarig at the head of Balquhidder Glen. He died there, peacefully, on the 28 December 1734. His funeral procession came down the 15-mile (24km) glen on New Years Day 1735 led by the MacGregor piper. His grave is beside the ruined church in front of the present Balquhidder parish church.

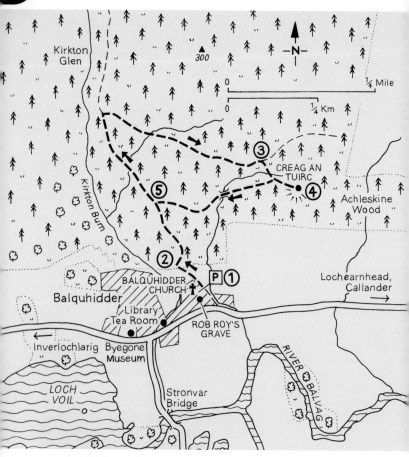

Walk 42 Directions

① From the car park at **Balquhidder church**, walk along a dirt track, go past a shed and cross a stile on the right-hand side which gives access to the forest. Follow the direction arrows on the green signposts pointing to Creag an Tuirc along a forest track and heading up the hill.

② Continue on this obvious trail for about ½ mile (800m) then turn right, beside a green building, again following the clearly signposted route along a forest road. After another ½ mile (800m) cross a gate on the right-hand side, go slightly downhill on some stone steps and across a small stream.

WHILE YOU'RE THERE　ⓘ

A short walk from Balquhidder church will bring you to a former laird's mansion overlooking Loch Voil. Inside is a smashing wee museum of everyday items from the past. The **Byegone Museum** has an eclectic collection of curio's, bric-à-brac and domestic utensils and equipment. And for children, particularly those in their forties, a superb range of old toys.

---

③ The path now heads uphill on some stone steps, through old pine trees and on towards the summit of a knoll. Here is a **cairn** erected by the Clan Maclaren Society in 1987 to commemorate their 25th anniversary. The plaque proclaims that this place is the ancient rallying point of their clan.

④ A seat below the cairn is a grand place to rest after the climb up here. Sit for a while and enjoy the superb views over the meandering line of the River Balvag and the length of Loch Voil with the Braes of Balquhidder rising steeply above it.

You can see the route that Rob Roy's funeral procession would have taken from Inverlochlarig down to the village itself, and the churchyard where his body lies. Now retrace your steps back down the hill but before reaching the top of the stone steps which you came up, take path to the left signposted 'Forest Walk'. This continues downhill following waymarked poles, down some steps and across a small bridge. The path goes through bracken, over a small stream and across a stile. Eventually it will pass through a small wood of young native trees before emerging on to the forest road.

⑤ Turn left here and retrace your steps back downhill over the stile and turn left to return to the car park. From here enter the churchyard and turn left. **Rob Roy's grave** is on the left in front of the ruins of a pre-Reformation church.

WHERE TO EAT AND DRINK　ⓘ

There's a small building in Balquhidder that was originally built as a library to keep the locals out of the pub. Now it is the **Library Tea Room** and serves excellent snacks and hot meals. Home-made soup, baked potatoes with a variety of fillings, toasties, sandwiches and cakes are all available to be washed down with a hot or cold drink.

WHAT TO LOOK FOR　ⓘ

The forest road continues past the junction where you turn off at the green building. Following this will take you on a longer walk up through the **Kirkton Glen** and into the hills on an ancient route to Glen Dochart where Rob Roy also had a house. Once up in these hills and amongst the heather it would have been impossible for soldiers to catch him.

Walk 43

The Shores of Loch Katrine

Glasgow's water supply in the heart of the Trossachs.

•DISTANCE•	6¾ miles (10.9km)
•MINIMUM TIME•	4hrs 30min
•ASCENT / GRADIENT•	420ft (128m) ▲▲▲
•LEVEL OF DIFFICULTY•	🚶🚶 🚶🚶 🚶🚶
•PATHS•	Water board roads, hill tracks
•LANDSCAPE•	Hills, woodland, lochs and heather
•SUGGESTED MAP•	aqua3 OS Explorers 364 Loch Lomond North; 365 The Trossachs
•START / FINISH•	Grid reference: NN 404102 (on Explorer 364)
•DOG FRIENDLINESS•	Keep on lead near loch and livestock
•PARKING•	Car park at Stronachlachar Pier
•PUBLIC TOILETS•	At car park

BACKGROUND TO THE WALK

Loch Katrine takes its name from the Gaelic 'cateran', a Highland robber – a fitting place then for the birthplace of Rob Roy MacGregor, the bandit, who was born at Glengyle at the western end of the loch. This is the heart of MacGregor country and one of their clan graveyards lies near the head of the loch (▶ Walk 42). Rob Roy's lasting fame is due to a novel of the same name written by Sir Walter Scott and the loch, too, owed its early popularity to one of Scott's poems, *The Lady of the Lake*. First published in 1810, Scott's description of the dramatic scenery encouraged tourists to visit the Trossachs. The poets Coleridge and Wordsworth were inspired by its beauty and Queen Victoria enjoyed a leisurely sail upon the loch in 1869. But the pure water of the loch was destined to be a crucial element in the growth of the City of Glasgow as well as a rural escape for its citizens.

By the start of the 19th century Glasgow's population of over 80,000, depended for their drinking water on a few public wells. Later, private companies supplied water from large barrels, selling it from the back of horse-drawn wagons. But the poor quality of the water, combined with dreadful overcrowding and poor sanitation, led to thousands of deaths from cholera in the 1830s and 40s.

By the mid-19th century Glasgow resolved to provide a municipal waterworks and commissioned John Frederick Bateman, an English engineer. Bateman identified Loch Katrine as the best source of water for Glasgow because of the quality of the water, the large catchment area and its remote, rural, location, but it required a massive feat of engineering. Bateman first built a large dam to raise the level of the loch. Then he constructed an aqueduct, 26 miles (41.8km) long to transport the water to a huge reservoir at Mugdock, on the outskirts of the city. A further 26 miles (41.8km) of main piping and 46 miles (74km) of distribution pipes were installed to take the water to all quarters of Glasgow.

After three and a half years of constant work, this marvel of engineering was officially opened by Queen Victoria in October 1859. Bateman himself was mightily impressed by his scheme and told the city fathers that he had left them 'a work which I believe will, with very slight attention, remain perfect for ages, which for the greater part of it, is indestructible as the hills through which it has been carried.'

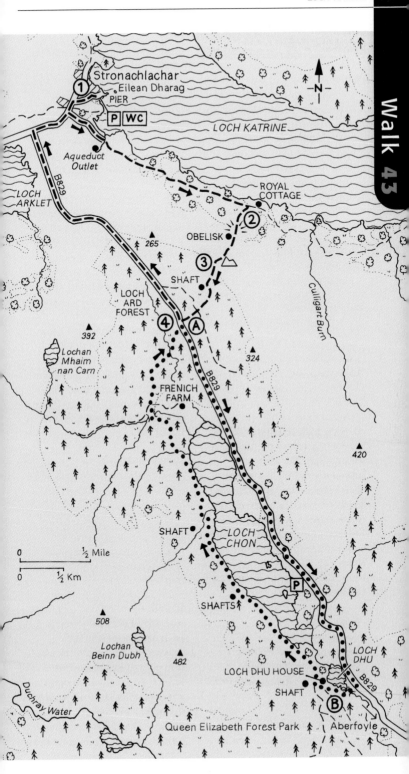

Walk 43

Walk 43 **Directions**

① From the car park follow the road back towards the **B829** and take the second turning on the left. This is an access road for Scottish Water vehicles only. Continue along the access road until you come to a cattle grid with green gate posts at the building known as **Royal Cottage**. Turn right just before this on to a rough gravel track that heads through some dense bracken.

WHAT TO LOOK FOR ⓘ

Just off the pier at Stronachlacher is **Eilean Dharag**, a small wooded island where Rob Roy MacGregor reputedly incarcerated Graham of Killearn, the Duke of Montrose's factor. Rob Roy had also taken the opportunity to relieve Graham of the rents he had been collecting for his master. Graham of Killearn succeeded in escaping, but not until Rob Roy was far away.

---

② As the path emerges on to open hillside you will see the first of several ventilation shafts and beyond it, on the hill, a strange obelisk. Follow the path along this line. When you reach the **obelisk** be sure to look back for a super view over Loch Katrine below and across to the hills with their narrow passes where Rob Roy and his men moved from Loch Katrine to Balquhidder and beyond, moving cattle or

---

WHERE TO EAT AND DRINK ⓘ

This is one of those occasions where a **picnic** is the only practical option. There are lots of excellent spots on the route to sit down, pour a cup of hot soup from your flask and enjoy your sandwiches while you gaze in awe at the scenery. Alternatively head back into Aberfoyle to the **Forth Inn** next to the car park there (► Walk 40).

---

escaping from the forces of law and order. Continue following the line of the ventilation shafts towards a chimney-like structure on top of a hill. From here go right and downhill. Take great care on this section as the path has eroded and is very steep. At the bottom, go through the gap at the junction of two fences. From here go left.

③ Follow a well-defined track that goes through some pine trees and past another ventilation shaft. Keep left at the shaft. It can be very muddy on this short stretch. Continue on the path until it intersects a forest road by a stream. Cross the road and look for a faint track continuing downhill in the same direction. In summer this path may be difficult to find because it's hidden by bracken. In this case follow the line of the telephone poles. Eventually after working downhill through more woodland the track emerges on to the **B829**.

WHILE YOU'RE THERE ⓘ

Head round to the Trossachs Pier and take a trip on the **SS *Sir Walter Scott***, the last of the screw-driven steamships in service on Scotland's inland waters. The trip sails via Stronachlachar and passes Royal Cottage, Ellen's Isle, the Factor's Island and Rob Roy's birthplace at Glelengyle House.

---

④ Turn right here and follow the road. It will eventually emerge from **Loch Ard Forest** into open countryside. Loch Arklet can be seen on the left; it is now connected to Loch Katrine by an underground pipeline. When the road reaches a T-junction with the Inversnaid road, turn right. When this road forks, turn right again and return to **Stronachlachar Pier**.

And on to Loch Dhu and Loch Chon

An easy and enjoyable walk, mainly on forest roads.
See map and information panel for Walk 43

•DISTANCE•	6 miles (9.7km)
•MINIMUM TIME•	3hrs
•ASCENT / GRADIENT•	33ft (10m) ▲ ▲▲ ▲▲
•LEVEL OF DIFFICULTY•	🚶 🚶 🚶

Walk 44 Directions
(Walk 43 option)

Turn left at Point Ⓐ and follow the road passing the **Loch Chon** (Loch of the Dogs) car park. From the car park the road goes inland a short way until it comes to **Loch Dhu** (the Black Loch). At the south end of this loch there's a road to the right leading to **Loch Dhu House** and also signposted to Rowardenen.

Both lochs are very picturesque and this easy and enjoyable walk is mainly on forestry roads. At first glance it would appear to have no connection with industrial archaeology but that's the primary function of this walk.

Cross a bridge (Point Ⓑ) and when the road reaches a T-junction look straight ahead for the outline of a ventilation shaft. Turn right and go uphill following the road along the banks of **Loch Chon**. Keep looking up to the left particularly where there are shafts or towers marked on your map. The latter are markers indicating the line of the mains water pipe from Loch Katrine which supplies water to Glasgow,

the former are ventilation shafts with large, well-like structures over them, sealed by huge iron grids.

In the 1930s large numbers of workers, and the unemployed, would use the pipe track as their main route out of Glasgow, following it on foot until they reached the Trossachs. They were hardy pioneering outdoor people who, with little or no equipment would spend the weekend climbing and exploring the hills, sleeping in the open, under a hedge or in what was left of the bothies and shelters that had been thrown up at the time when the pipeline was built.

Follow this road along the banks of the loch, cross a bridge and pass the turn off to **Frenich Farm**. To your right are more ventilation shafts. These continue in a line across the road marking the route of the pipe all the way to Royal Cottage on the banks of Loch Katrine. It was near Royal Cottage that Queen Victoria opened the sluice gates to start the flow of water to Glasgow in 1859. As you approach the end of the forest road go through a gate to a T-junction with the **B829**. Turn left and continue to rejoin the main route (Point Ⓐ).

Walk 45

Rest and Be Thankful

A steep climb up one of Scotland's most famous military roads.

•DISTANCE•	4½ miles (7.2km)
•MINIMUM TIME•	3hrs
•ASCENT / GRADIENT•	426ft (130m) ▲▲▲
•LEVEL OF DIFFICULTY•	🚶🚶 🚶🚶 🚶🚶
•PATHS•	Forest roads and metalled road, 4 stiles
•LANDSCAPE•	Hills, glen and forest
•SUGGESTED MAP•	aqua3 OS Explorer 364 Loch Lomond North
•START / FINISH•	Grid reference: NN 230073
•DOG FRIENDLINESS•	Keep on lead near livestock
•PARKING•	Rest and Be Thankful car park
•PUBLIC TOILETS•	None on route

Walk 45 Directions

Prior to the 17th century the Highlands of Scotland were a remote area and, for all practical purposes, inaccessible. Rough drove roads or paths followed the line of glens and rivers and most travel was by foot or on horseback. England had roads dating back to the time of the Romans but there were few roads in Scotland and none at all in the Highlands. Continuing political unrest in the Highlands led the government to dispatch General George Wade to Scotland in 1724. He was charged with pacifying the region. Like the Romans, Wade concluded that an intensive programme of road building would allow the rapid deployment of troops and supplies and enable the army to instigate a greater measure of control.

From the **marker stone** in the car park, commemorating the renovation of this particular stretch of military road, veer left on to a track leading uphill and away from the road. Turn left on to the **B828**, continue along this road then turn left on to a forest road with a waymark indicating hill access to Ben Donich.

Wade was appointed Commander-in-Chief Scotland and between 1726 and 1737 he built over 250 miles (402km) of roads through the Highlands. Construction, all of it by soldiers, was hard, back-breaking work. First the turf would be removed and the topsoil, then the soldiers would dig until they hit rock or stone. This was levelled using a sledgehammer or, if the stones proved to be too large, they would be blasted with powder or

---

WHERE TO EAT AND DRINK ⓘ

This is an excellent walk to indulge in a picnic but just in case the weather is unsuitable there's a wee white **caravan** in the car park at the Rest and Be Thankful where two exceedingly friendly people spend their day dispensing hot drinks, home-made soup, filled rolls, sandwiches, cakes and biscuits. It's open all year round and also seems to double as the canteen for the local traffic police.

levered out of the ground. To complete the job, 18in (45cm) of gravel would be laid on top of the foundation, this would be compacted by boots and spades and then the topsoil removed earlier was used to build the retaining banks. Finally ditches were dug to ensure good drainage and to keep the surface free from flooding. On a good day an average soldier could construct 4ft 6in (1.37m) of road.

WHILE YOU'RE THERE

Hillhouse, in Hellensburgh, is the finest of Charles Rennie Macintosh's houses. Designed by him for Walter Blackie, the Glasgow publisher, it sits on an imposing site overlooking the Clyde. Macintosh also designed the furniture, interior fittings and decorative schemes as well as the house and garden. His wife, Margaret MacDonald, produced a gesso overmantel and fabric designs.

WHAT TO LOOK FOR

Check along the line of the military road to see if you can spot the line of **banks** constructed from the removed topsoil and the remains of ditches dug by Major Caulfield's soldiers. You might also come across the odd section of road where the tarmac surface is worn through to the original surface below and get some idea of how rough these former 'state-of-the-art' roads were.

Turn left at the next waymarker and continue on another forest road. Go through a gate and continue until you reach a fork in the road. Go left, continuing along forestry roads with a superb view of the old military road below you to the left.

Wade's roads were a huge success, but not initially as he had imagined. During the 1745 Jacobite rising, Bonnie Prince Charlie used Wade's roads to move his own forces south at a rapid pace, defeating all before him. He got as far as Derby and it is conceivable that had he continued to London the House of Hanover would have fallen. However, taking bad advice, he retreated instead of advancing and was eventually defeated at Culloden in 1746.

The forest road heads steadily downhill then turns left on to a bridge over the **Croe Water**. At the T-junction just after the bridge, turn left again on to the **Old Military Road**. This section was once the main road here until the A83 was built higher up the hillside, so the surface is relatively modern, unlike other sections of military road found elsewhere in Scotland. Go through a gate, then cross a stile at another and continue along the road, which is fairly flat at this point, but in the distance you will see it climb up, back to the car park.

After Culloden, Wade's former assistant Major William Caulfield continued the programme of road building. He began his work in Argyll in 1746 and, up until his death in 1767, Caulfield built over 800 miles (1,287km) of roads, over three times the amount constructed by his former boss yet it is Wade's name that is still linked to those early roads.

Caulfield continued to work on the Dumbarton to Inveraray road in 1747 and the following year his men reached the summit of the Rest and Be Thankful. As you cross the last two stiles then follow the road as it turns and climbs steeply to the car park, you'll realise why it bears that name. At the top cross a stile to arrive back in the car park and the stone erected in 1768 by the soldiers who repaired this section.

Walked with David on Sunday 10th October 2004
Lovely walk!

Walk 46

From Puck's Glen to the Benmore Botanic Garden

The story of James Duncan the man who altered the Cowal landscape.

•DISTANCE•	4 miles (6.4km)
•MINIMUM TIME•	2hrs 30min
•ASCENT / GRADIENT•	459ft (140m) ▲▲▲
•LEVEL OF DIFFICULTY•	栋栋 栋栋 栋栋
•PATHS•	Mainly forest roads and well-made footpaths, 1 stile
•LANDSCAPE•	Woodland
•SUGGESTED MAP•	aqua3 OS Explorer 363 Cowal East
•START / FINISH•	Grid reference: NS 142855
•DOG FRIENDLINESS•	Keep dogs on lead
•PARKING•	Car park at Benmore Botanic Garden
•PUBLIC TOILETS•	At Benmore Botanic Garden

BACKGROUND TO THE WALK

Better-known as the Younger Botanic Garden, after Harry George Younger who gifted his estate to the nation in 1925, the Benmore Botanic Garden is 120 acres (48.5ha) of the former estate. Extensive development, since it became part of the Royal Botanic Garden, Edinburgh, has made it world famous for its plant collections. The remainder of the estate, including Puck's Glen, belongs to the Forestry Commission and their afforested hillsides provide a splendid backdrop to the garden's formal collections. Yet none of this would exist without the passionate commitment of a self-made Victorian merchant, James Duncan.

Transforming the Landscape

Duncan, who made his fortune from sugar refining at Greenock, purchased the Benmore Estate in 1870 and laid the foundations of the gardens. When Duncan came to Benmore the landscape was bare and uninteresting. He immediately extended the former Tower House to create the main part of Benmore House. Around the formal gardens he constructed countless ranges of heated glasshouses and, overhanging a ravine in Glen Massan, he established a fernery, the remains of which are still visible today. Acting on the advice of Sir Joseph Hooker, Director of the Royal Botanic Gardens at Kew, Duncan began to plant the collections of shrubs and trees, which would provide the basis of the gardens.

Cowal's Golden Gates

Extensive drainage systems were developed throughout the estate and trees were planted on the bare hillsides. Between 1871 and 1883 Duncan planted some 1,600 acres (648ha). The total area stretched from the Strone of Clyde to the head of Loch Eck. When he had done there were a total of 6,480,000 trees, which remain a major feature of the present landscape of this part of the Cowal peninsula.

Duncan also commissioned the Golden Gates for the Paris Exhibition of 1865. Made from wrought iron and painted gold with his initials worked into them, they were eventually erected near Glen Massan in 1873. A sociable man, Duncan entertained frequently and welcomed many visitors to Benmore, including Sir Henry Morton Stanley, the explorer, and Charles Haddon Spurgeon, the Billy Graham of his day, who preached to a crowd of 7,000 in the grounds of Benmore in 1877.

Lasting Memorial
Duncan died at Spean Bridge, near Fort William on 12 August 1905, aged 81. His body was brought back to Cowal and is buried in the historic churchyard at Kilmun. His body lies under a pink granite slab on a high part of the steep graveyard with a view looking across the Holy Loch. At the southern limit of his Kilmun estate, on the Strone peninsula at Graham's Point, an obelisk was erected to Duncan's memory and on it can be found the only known likeness of the man, carved in stone. But his real memorial is the garden at Benmore and the surrounding landscape.

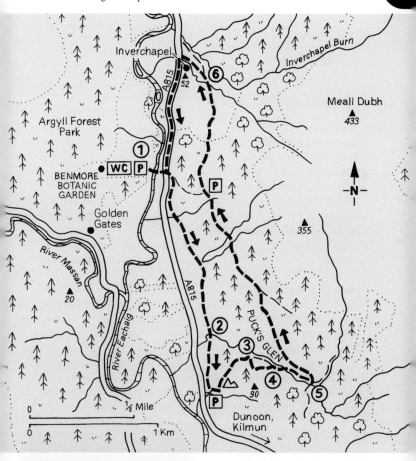

Walk 46 **Directions**

① From the car park cross the **A815** and follow the footpath past a waymarker for Black Gates. Pass a sign for the Big Tree Walk and turn right on to a surfaced lane. Continue along this lane for about 1 mile (1.6km) and just after the parapet of a bridge is the first footpath to **Puck's Glen** on the left.

② There's a milestone here pointing to Dunoon Pier 6 miles. Ignore this entrance and continue along the lane until you reach the car park. Turn left and along a footpath past the waymarker pole for Puck's Glen 4.8 miles (3km). Climb uphill on a steep path.

WHAT TO LOOK FOR ⓘ
With care and if you are quiet, you may spot a **red squirrel** scurrying about in the trees. It's the only species of squirrel native to Britain and is gradually being forced out by the larger American grey squirrel. Red squirrel populations have been in decline since the 1940s owing to competition from the grey for food. Now they are found mainly in Scotland, northern England and parts of Wales.

③ At the top of the hill the path levels out then starts to head back downhill, rather steeply on a series of steps with handrails to the bottom of the gorge. A signpost at a junction at the bottom of the steps points left for the lower gorge and right for the upper.

④ Turn right, head downhill on another set of steps then cross a bridge on the left and turn right to head along a footpath on the opposite side of the stream. Head uphill, cross another bridge then go past a series of small waterfalls. Eventually reach yet another bridge to cross before coming to a set of steps that takes you up a steep part of the hillside to another bridge at the top. After crossing it the path levels out a bit and continues through the trees to reach a T-junction with a forestry road.

⑤ At the junction is a waymarker and signpost. Turning right will lead you along a forest road to **Kilmun Arboretum**. However, for this walk you must turn left, following the signs for Black Gates. Because of ongoing forestry operations and renovations to several of the footpaths, diversions may be in place or footpaths may simply be closed.

⑥ Follow the signs to the left and go on to the path for Black Gates car park and, from there, return to the botanic gardens. Otherwise continue on the forest road until you reach a gate near its end. Cross a stile then turn left at the T-junction on to the **A815**. Walk along here for ½ mile (800m) to return to the start.

WHERE TO EAT AND DRINK ⓘ
The excellent tea room at the **Benmore Botanic Garden** can be accessed from the car park without having to pay for admission to the grounds. It's a spacious and delightful area with large glass windows on all sides giving grand views of the fabulous array of trees and shrubs outside and the variety of birds that feed at strategically sited bird tables. The tea room staff are very friendly and the food is of a high quality.

WHILE YOU'RE THERE ⓘ
Head out of Dunoon on the Sandbank road for a visit to the **Cowal Bird Garden**. Not only do they have a large number of exotic birds on display but also some friendly pets to entertain the children. Geese, ducks, parrots and macaws can be seen along with ornamental pheasant and rheas. Goats, pot-bellied pigs, donkeys and a wonderful wee Shetland pony are the animal representatives.

First climbed, with Benny & Romy, on a beautiful late afternoon 23/5/04. Dinner afterwards @ Loch Fyne Oyster Bar

Along the Crinan Canal and Around Mhoine Mhor

A lengthy but easy stroll along a 19th-century canal and around Scotland's last wild peat bog.

•DISTANCE•	8¼ miles (13.3km)
•MINIMUM TIME•	5hrs
•ASCENT / GRADIENT•	176ft (55m)
•LEVEL OF DIFFICULTY•	
•PATHS•	Canal tow path, country roads and farm tracks
•LANDSCAPE•	Bog, hillside and pasture
•SUGGESTED MAP•	aqua3 OS Explorer 358 Lochgilphead & Knapdale North
•START / FINISH•	Grid reference: NR 824908
•DOG FRIENDLINESS•	Keep on lead near livestock
•PARKING•	Dunardry Forest car park
•PUBLIC TOILETS•	None on route

BACKGROUND TO THE WALK

Built just over 200 years ago the Crinan Canal, a mere 9 miles (14.5km) in length, with just 15 locks, allows easy passage from Loch Fyne to the Sound of Jura, avoiding the lengthy voyage around the Mull of Kintyre. It was designed by John Rennie but later improved by Thomas Telford in about 1817. Because it is 69ft (21m) above sea level it needs a constant supply of water to replenish it and its main channels are fed from seven reservoirs in the hills above. But as every single locking operation uses 66,000 gallons (300,000 litres) of water, there have been periods, particularly during long dry summers when it has run out of water and been forced to close.

The Great Moss
The Crinan Canal runs along the southern fringe of Moine Mhor, the Great Moss, one of the last wild, raised bogs remaining in Britain and one of the oldest living sphagnum bogs in Europe. As plants die, their remains become peat. Older than Stonehenge but growing at a rate of only 1mm each year, Moine Mhor is 13ft (4m) in depth and is protected as part of a National Nature Reserve.

Abundant Birdlife
The moss can be visited at any time. A wooden walkway leads from the North Moss car park area and this is the best way to view it. It's a birdwatchers' paradise echoing with the distinctive cry of the curlew as it returns to breed each spring. Stonechats, resident year round, are joined by whinchats in summer and you may spot the odd osprey hunting fish in the River Add. Watch too for the hen harrier quartering the moss in search of a quick meal. During the seasons the bog changes colour as heathers and grasses bloom then fade away. Cranberries bear purple flowers in the spring and deep red berries in autumn. Carnivorous plants like the bright green sundew plants lie in wait to catch unsuspecting insects in their sticky hairs.

Invaders from Ireland

In AD 500 the Scotti tribe from Antrim landed here. To the Scotti, the vast rock of Dunadd in the middle of this great bog would have been the obvious place on which to build their first fortress and settlement. So the rock became the early capital of Dalriada. Near the summit are rock carvings including the figure of a boar, which may have been the tribe's emblem and some faint lines of ogam (alphabet of straight lines) inscription. A basin and footprint carved from the rock were probably part of early coronation ceremonies. The first recorded coronation here was of Aedann mac Gabhran by St Columba in AD 574. Dunadd, capital of Dalriada until 900, is still regarded as one of the most important historic sites in Scotland.

Walk 47 **Directions**

① From the car park go down some steps, cross the road and turn left. Keep going until you reach a white cottage on your right. Turn right and on to a dirt track that runs behind the cottage then go

through a gap between the fence and a wall. Cross the canal over **Dunardry Lock** and turn left on to the tow path.

② Head along the tow path as far as **Bellanoch Bridge** then turn right on to the road, cross **Islandadd Bridge** and on to the **B8025**. This narrow, but not busy, road is long and straight and runs right through the **Moine Mhor**. Keep going for nearly 2 miles (3.2km) then turn right on to an unclassified road signposted for Drimvore.

③ Follow this for about 1¾ miles (2.8km) as it runs through the National Nature Reserve and passes the farms of **Dalvore** and **Drimvore**. Finally reach a T-junction with the **A816** and turn right. After ½ mile (800m) an Historic Scotland fingerpost will point you in the direction of Dunadd Fort.

④ Turn right here on to a long straight farm road and keep on it, passing the farm of **Dunadd**, until your reach the Historic Scotland car park. Make your way towards the hill on a well-trodden path, go past the house on the left and through a kissing gate. Continue on the path,

following the directions arrows, to emerge through a gap in some rocks within the outer ramparts.

⑤ Continue from here to the summit and after you have admired the views, seen the carvings and tried your own foot in the carved footprint, return by the same route to the car park. Leave it and turn right on to a farm track. Go through a gate then, almost immediately, go left through another gate and follow it as it curves left.

⑥ Another gate is encountered just before the road turns right and heads uphill. Continue following the road going through another gate until you reach the steading of **Dunamuck farm**. Turn left through the steading, go through a gate and head downhill on a farm road, continuing on it until you reach a T-junction with the **A816**.

⑦ Turn right on to the road and follow it for about ½ mile (800m) then turn right on to an unclassified road signposted from the **Cairnbaan Hotel**. After ¼ mile (400m) turn right on to the **B841** towards Crinan. As the road turns left across the swing bridge keep straight ahead and on to the canal tow path. Follow this back to **Dunardry Lock** and retrace your steps to the car park.

Walk 48

The Neolithic Monuments of Kilmartin Glen

A short walk back in time to the stone shrines and monuments in the valley of the ghosts.

•DISTANCE•	3½ miles (5.7km)
•MINIMUM TIME•	3hrs
•ASCENT / GRADIENT•	Negligible
•LEVEL OF DIFFICULTY•	
•PATHS•	Boggy fields, old coach road and country lanes, 3 stiles
•LANDSCAPE•	Pasture, hills, woodland
•SUGGESTED MAP•	aqua3 OS Explorer 358 Lochgilphead & Knapdale North
•START / FINISH•	Grid reference: NR 835988
•DOG FRIENDLINESS•	Dogs fine on route
•PARKING•	Car park outside Kilmartin church
•PUBLIC TOILETS•	Kilmartin House

BACKGROUND TO THE WALK

Kilmartin Glen with its lush alluvial plains, easy landfalls on the coast near Crinan and an abundant supply of water has attracted human settlers since the earliest times. In around 5000 BC, nomadic hunter gatherers frequented this area but left little evidence of their presence other than piles of bones and shells in caves.

Early Settlers

The arrival of small groups of neolithic people from around 3000 BC provided the first lasting signs of habitation. These early settlers, farmers and skilled weavers and potters, cleared the ground for grazing and erected the first stone shrines and circles. What these standing stones were for no one knows for certain, but they were probably an early form of astronomical calendar for determining when to plant and harvest crops or to move cattle. They were probably also part of religious rituals closely related to the seasons and survival. Around Kilmartin Glen 25 different sites of standing stones have been found. Some are simple arrangements, others single stones, while in Temple Wood the monument consists of two stone circles.

Great Monuments

Later, Bronze-Age people were responsible for the great monuments that can still be seen in the fascinating prehistoric linear cemetery, built over the course of 1,000 years, that runs for a mile (1.6km) down the glen. Each of the huge stone-lined burial chambers is slightly different in design and construction.

The Glebe Cairn, which looks like a pile of boulders with a cap stone, is situated near the church and is typical of the burial cairns of the period 1700–1500 BC. At the centre of this cairn were two stone cists for the burials and these contained pottery and a necklace of jet beads. The next tomb south from here, known as the North Tomb, has been rebuilt over a modern shelter that allows access through a hatch and contains a large slab carved with pictures of axe heads and cupmarks. The last cairn in this direction, the South Cairn is the earliest and was originally a chambered tomb dating from 4000 BC.

In the Iron Age, warring tribes ringed the glen with hill forts and it was on one of these, at Dunadd, that the Scotti tribe from Ireland founded their capital in the 6th century AD (▶ Walk 47). St Columba came to Kilmartin in the 6th century AD and is believed to have established the first Christian church here.

Within Kilmartin parish church can be found relics from a later age. The ornately carved Kilmartin Cross depicts one of the most moving images of Christ to have survived from the early Scottish Christian Church and the churchyard has one of the finest collections of ornately carved medieval gravestones in Scotland.

Walk 48 Directions

① From the car park visit **Kilmartin church** to view the stones and the Kilmartin Cross. Leave the church, turn left and walk along the road past **Kilmartin**

House, exit the village and head downhill towards a garage on the left. Just before the garage turn left, go through a kissing gate and head across the field to the **Glebe Cairn**.

② From the cairn head half right, across the field to cross a stile. In wet weather this can be very boggy so stout footwear is advisable. Cross the stream by a bridge. Go through a gate and turn left on to the old coach road. Follow this to the next cairn. Go left over a stile and follow the path to visit the cairn.

③ Return to the road and turn left, continuing to the next cairn. After exploring this, follow the coach road to Kilmartin school, where the route becomes a metalled road. Go through a crossroads, past **Nether Largie farm** and, ignoring the cairn on the left, continue a short distance to **Temple Wood** ahead on the right.

WHERE TO EAT AND DRINK

One of the problems of walking in Scotland is finding everything has shut when you need a meal. Kilmartin unfortunately falls into this category. However a few miles south on the A816, the **Horseshoe Inn** at Bridgend is family-friendly, open for wonderful food all day, seven days a week and even managed to serve up a splendid lunch during a power cut.

④ Go through a gate on the right into Temple Wood, then return by the same route. Turn right on to the road and continue until you reach a T-junction. Turn left and walk along this road until you come to a sign on the right for **Ri Cruin Cairn**. Cross the wall via a stile and proceed along the well-defined path to the ancient monument.

⑤ Return by the same route and turn right on to the road. Follow it to a T-junction then turn left and keep straight ahead until you reach the car park at **Lady Glassary Wood**. Opposite this take a path to the left signposted to Temple Wood. Cross a bridge, go through a gate,

WHILE YOU'RE THERE

Inveraray Jail is one of the most popular attractions in Argyll. Last used in 1930 this ostentatious Georgian courthouse with its prison cells is now an award-winning museum. Within the cells actors recreate the harsh reality of life in the Duke of Argyll's jail. Within the courtroom itself visitors can sit in the public benches and listen to snippets from some of the trials that took place there.

cross another bridge and head towards the standing stones.

⑥ Turn right and walk across the field away from the stones towards a wood. Go through a gate and follow the fenced path to **Nether Largie Cairn**. From here continue along the fenced path, go through another gate and turn right on to the road. Continue past **Nether Largie farm** and Kilmartin school and then retrace your steps back to **Kilmartin church** and the car park.

WHAT TO LOOK FOR

Look out for the **carvings** on the tomb stones in Kilmartin church. Intricate Celtic designs indicate an Irish influence on the work of local sculptors or that the sculptors themselves had come from Ireland. Others bear the effigy of armed knights carved in relief. Above the door in the church you'll find what was once the side slab of a tomb chest.

Walk 49

On To New Poltalloch

A walk to the faded ruin of a Victorian state-of-the-art dream.
See map and information panel for Walk 48

•DISTANCE•	6¼ miles (10.1km)
•MINIMUM TIME•	4hrs 30min
•ASCENT / GRADIENT•	Negligible
•LEVEL OF DIFFICULTY•	

Walk 49 Directions
(Walk 48 option)

On reaching the T-junction at Point **Ⓐ**, go straight ahead, past the **lodge cottage** on your right and proceed along a dilapidated estate road. Turn right at a T-junction and walk along this road, through stone gate posts next to a church.

The **Church of St Columba** was built in 1854 by the noted English church architect Thomas Cundy, Junior. It's his only work in Scotland and had stained-glass windows by William Wailes.

Continue along the main drive towards **New Poltalloch house**. At a bend in the drive, just before the large white **Gardeners House**, search on the left for an overgrown junction where the road branches off to the big house. Duck under the overgrown rhododendrons and continue until you reach a ruined building. Turn left and follow an overgrown path to a gate that exits into a field. Veer right and cross to the front entrance of the old house.

This enormous pile was built in 1849, in the neo-Jacobean style, by the famous Scottish architect

William Burn. the most sought after architect of his time and a pioneer of the Scots Baronial style. It cost Neil Malcolm, the owner, £100,000 – a colossal sum at the time – yet it stood for just over 100 years. Originally it was called Calltuinn Mór, the place of the great hazel trees, to distinguish it from the previous Poltalloch but soon became known as New Polltalloch.

Do not under any circumstances go inside the old house. The floors have gone and the interior is unsafe. When you have finished looking at it return to the front, go though a gate and follow the rough road to another gate, go through it and continue on the estate road ahead.

Looking back along the track for a splendid view of the ruin, its walls intact but with grasses, plants and trees growing from them and from the interior. By the 1950s the house was no longer, in 1957 the roof was removed to avoid high taxes and in no time the building was effectively dead.

Follow the road through the estate until it reaches a T-junction beside **East Lodge**. Turn left on to the main road and walk along it to the next junction (Point **Ⓑ**) where you will rejoin the main walk.

Walk 50

Carradale Forest Walk

A gentle stroll above the home of Naomi Mitchison.

•DISTANCE•	6 miles (9.7km)
•MINIMUM TIME•	3hrs
•ASCENT / GRADIENT•	410ft (125m) ▲▲▲
•LEVEL OF DIFFICULTY•	林 林 林
•PATHS•	Forest roads, some forest paths and shingle beach, 1 stile
•LANDSCAPE•	Forest, hillside, beach, pasture
•SUGGESTED MAP•	aqua3 OS Explorer 356 Kintyre South
•START / FINISH•	Grid reference: NR 801381
•DOG FRIENDLINESS•	Good walk for dogs
•PARKING•	Network Carradale Visitor Centre
•PUBLIC TOILETS•	At visitor centre

Walk 50 Directions

Carradale, on the Mull of Kintyre, is where novelist Naomi Mitchison (1897–1999) and her husband Dick came to live in 1937. They bought Carradale House and Naomi spent most of her life here. A prolific writer, she continued to work well into her 80s and died at Carradale when she was 101.

From the **visitor centre** go past the interpretation boards, up wooden steps and turn left at the green waymarker pole. Go uphill through a wood then turn left where the path meets a forest road. Follow the blue and red waymarker poles.

Mitcheson was born in Edinburgh in 1897, educated at the Dragon School, Oxford and following in the footsteps of her famous father, the physiologist, J B S Haldane, went on to the university to read science. She abandoned her studies to enter nursing and in 1916 married Dick Mitcheson, a barrister and, later, Labour politician.

Pass the waymarked turning for the red walk and continue along the forest road for about a mile (1.6km). Look out for some unusual shrubs including quince bushes and a profusion of wild flowers, particularly red campion, growing by the side of the road. Eventually reach a gate across the road. Cross here by a stile to arrive at a car park which is an alternative start to the walk.

When the Mitchisons lived in London, their house at Hammersmith was famous for its hospitality. The list of their visitors and friends reads like the literary Who's Who of the day and included Adlous Huxley, E M Forster, A P Herbert and Wyndham Lewis. When they moved to Carradale the

---

WHILE YOU'RE THERE

Don't miss the fascinating displays at the **Network Carradale Visitor Centre** which chart the history of the area from prehistoric times to the present day. The sea and fishing are both covered in depth and it's the best place to come to learn about the local wildlife and forestry.

parties continued and it was not unusual for Naomi to be found typing away on an old battered typewriter surrounded by an army of visitors and children.

Turn right at the car park and follow the blue waymarkers on an old farm track uphill. When the track rejoins the forest road keep right. The road climbs uphill from here to reach the highest point of the walk with magnificent views over the sea to Arran.

> **WHAT TO LOOK FOR** ⓘ
> Look across the water to **Arran**. From the forest road above the beach and the beach itself you will have a clear view of where the Highland Boundary Fault divides the island with the hilly, Highland area to your left and the flatter Lowlands to the right.

Naomi wrote over 90 books on a variety of subjects ranging from Arthurian legend to science fiction. In her most controversial work, *We Have Been Wanted*, this noted feminist explored the whole gamut of sexual behaviour including rape. Rejected by several publishers and subjected to censorship it was published in 1935.

Continue on this forest road until it ends, then continue on a footpath following the blue waymark poles. The path enters the forest then heads rather steeply downhill. Care needs to be taken on this section, particularly when it has been wet.

Actively involved in the local community Naomi represented the area on the local council and was responsible for instigating the improvements to the village harbour. Although Carradale House was regarded as an intellectual

centre for the leading young left-wing men and women of the time, Naomi had a wide circle of friends drawn from all sections of society, and there was every possibility that they would find themselves in the company of ghillies, fishermen and locals from the village.

Continue downhill and after the last section on a series of steps pass by some unusual rock formations and exit the forest on to the shore. Turn right and continue along the shingle beach for about 200yds (183m). Watch carefully for the next waymarker which is partially concealed in the trees.

Naomi was awarded a life peerage for her services to literature in 1964 but probably valued her appointment as 'mother' and advisor to the Baktgatla tribe of Botswana more.

> **WHERE TO EAT AND DRINK** ⓘ
> The **tea room** at the visitor centre serves satisfying home-made soups, sandwiches and a host of hot main meals and, snacks. It also doubles as a gift shop for local souvenirs.

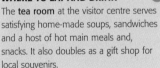

Re-enter the forest and pick your way carefully across an often mucky and uneven path. This enters and leaves the forest several times until, finally, you leave the beach and head uphill on a steep path and steps. At the top turn left at a blue waymarker on to a forest road. There is a good view over Carradale from here. **Carradale House** is hidden by trees, privately owned it is not open to the public.

Continue following the waymarkers to the sign for the **Network Centre**. Turn left here and return to the visitor centre.

Walking in Safety

All these walks are suitable for any reasonably fit person, but less experienced walkers should try the easier walks first. Route finding is usually straightforward, but you will find that an Ordnance Survey map is a useful addition to the route maps and descriptions.

Risks

Although each walk here has been researched with a view to minimising the risks to the walkers who follow its route, no walk in the countryside can be considered to be completely free from risk. Walking in the outdoors will always require a degree of common sense and judgement to ensure that it is as safe as possible.

- Be particularly careful on cliff paths and in upland terrain, where the consequences of a slip can be very serious.

- Remember to check tidal conditions before walking on the seashore.

- Some sections of route are by, or cross, busy roads. Take care and remember traffic is a danger even on minor country lanes.

- Be careful around farmyard machinery and livestock, especially if you have children with you.

- Be aware of the consequences of changes in the weather and check the forecast before you set out. Carry spare clothing and a torch if you are walking in the winter months. Remember the weather can change very quickly at any time of the year, and in moorland and heathland areas, mist and fog can make route finding much harder. Don't set out in these conditions unless you are confident of your navigation skills in poor visibility. In summer remember to take account of the heat and sun; wear a hat and carry spare water.

- On walks away from centres of population you should carry a whistle and survival bag. If you do have an accident requiring the emergency services, make a note of your position as accurately as possible and dial 999.

Acknowledgements

Hugh Taylor and Moira McCrossan would like to thank Moira Dyer of Glasgow and Clyde Valley Tourist Board and Mike Blair of Caledonian MacBrayne for facilities and information. Archibald W Taylor and George Hood for background information on shepherds and the lace industry and David Hunter FSA Scot for information on Kirsty McTaggart.

AQUA3 AA Publishing and Outcrop Publishing Services would like to thank Chartech for supplying aqua3 maps for this book.
For more information visit their website: www.aqua3.com.

Series management: Outcrop Publishing Services Limited, Cumbria
Series editor: Chris Bagshaw **Copy editor:** Pam Stagg
Front cover: AA Photo Library/S Day **Back cover:** AA Photo Library/J Martin